Editorial

The Scourge of the Scriptures?

CAROL WARDMAN

If you're looking for a classical work on ethics which might best inform twenty-first century attitudes to women and gender-based violence, it's probably fair to say that the Bible is not the first book that springs to mind. From treating women as property conveyanced from fathers to husbands, and compensating fathers or husbands for the damages incurred by rape, to an emphasis on extreme forgiveness and the prohibition of divorce at all costs, neither the Hebrew Bible nor the New Testament appears to fare very well by standards of modern scrutiny.

Attitudes change. As contributors to the debate here testify, we recognize all sorts of atrocities from the past that weren't such a big deal at the time. Within recent memory, there was no such thing as rape within marriage; police hesitated to attend callouts for assaults in the home, because they were 'domestic matters'; celebrities and community leaders are now being prosecuted for sexual offences which were regarded at the time as normal behaviour, harmless pranks, or disregarded because they happened to excitable teenage girls. We re-examine all sorts of historical events and attitudes, and the Bible should not be uniquely excluded.

One of the things the Bible teaches us is that if there is a difficult, painful or even dangerous issue to be dealt with, the first thing we have to do is face it head-on. That's what the Israelites in the wilderness had to do when they suffered an infestation of poisonous snakes: if they were bitten, Moses told them to look up at a model of a snake on a stick, and by facing it, they gained the strength to recover. That is often paralleled with contemplating Jesus on the cross: we see there an example of the worst suffering that human beings can inflict on one another. It isn't something we want to think about; but the only way we can hope to deal with it is to face it unflinchingly.

And that's where we have to start with violence against

women. So, in this edition of *Crucible* we encounter a variety of perspectives on the worldwide scourge that afflicts at least one in three of the women alive today.

Peggy Jackson recounts her experiences of encountering women in abusive situations, and how the Church gradually progressed in its understanding and ability to help, partly through the introduction to sacramental ministry of women priests embodying a new and fuller understanding of humanity in the image of God. Simon Prince mirrors some of these experiences as he describes how Dyfed-Powys Police strive to improve their response to domestic violence. Mandy Marshall of *Restored*, an international Christian alliance to transform relationships and end violence against women, shows how the Church itself is not immune to perpetrating and covering up the problem, explodes some myths and makes practical suggestions for how churches can become part of the solution. Alan Paterson reflects on how some constructions of masculinity derived from traditional work and family role models, plus ignorance and misunderstanding about sex and relationships, might contribute to a crisis which embraces crime, domestic violence and the sex industry. Cathrin Daniel introduces the international perspective, linking the violence of sexual assault, Female Genital Mutilation and female mortality with the structural violence of inequality and poverty.

According to one version of the Creation story, man was made first, and then woman. Man was made directly by God out of the stuff of the earth; woman was secondary, inherently inferior. Falling from grace in Eden was the woman's fault; and after the Fall, Eve is told by God that from now on, her primary aim in life will be to get and please her man: 'your desire will be for your husband'; and he will be her 'master'/'ruler' (Gen. 3.16). Female virginity commanded a high premium, but the same level of purity did not seem to be required of men. A bride could be stoned for being suspected of pre-marital sex; but the accusation was serious enough that to falsely accuse a woman of sleeping with someone else before the wedding was not grounds for adultery. All this based on evidence of wedding-night virginity, carefully preserved by the wife's father. Visiting a prostitute attracted no censure, but 'playing the harlot in your father's house' (Gen. 38.24) was a disgrace. Convictions for rape rather depended on whether or not you had been heard screaming in a built-up area; and if we think it's bad for a rape victim to have to face her assailant in court, according to Exodus 22 the law required a woman to marry her rapist. Men were allowed to divorce their wives for various reasons, but even if that post-rape marriage didn't work out, women were never allowed to initiate divorce proceedings (Deut. 24).

Uncomfortable as it is to admit, the New Testament also displays a worrying level of inequality. Jesus' strengthening of the divorce laws (preventing even men from initiating proceedings) is reinforced numerous times in the Epistles. 1 Corinthians 7 states that a woman is 'bound' to her husband for life: no divorce, no escape, or at the very least, no second chance of happiness in a new marriage.

The household codes of the Epistles describe the man as the head of the woman as Christ is the head of the Church. Women should accept the authority of their husbands and submit to them (Ephesians, Colossians and 1 Corinthians); and it's even strongly hinted that it's more virtuous for women, like slaves, to accept unfair treatment, including beatings, more uncomplainingly than if they were treated properly. 'In the same way', says Peter, 'wives must submit ...' (1 Pet. 3.1, closely following 1 Pet. 2.19–20).

But before we all throw away our Bibles in a surge of righteous feminist indignation, it may be worth a more careful look at those all- too-well-known proof texts. Strangely enough, they may not say quite what the vested interests of powerful groups down the millennia have tried to make us think they say.

In the first account of Creation, Adam is not made first, with Eve as an afterthought. Even that rib story should more properly be seen as describing the woman as the man's equal, made of exactly the same stuff as him, except that the Hebrew word *ezer* (helper or partner) is most often applied in the Bible to the role of God coming to the aid of hapless humanity. The imbalance of power where the husband rules over his wife is not a creation ordinance: the gloomy prognosis after the Fall is a symptom and consequence of sin.

Alongside the list of matrimonial causes in Deuteronomy 24 are safeguards to protect divorced women from abuse and destitution. In Malachi 2.16 we have a rare biblical reference to partner abuse when we learn that God regards divorce as an abhorrent offence for husbands to commit against their wives, along with infidelity and domestic violence: 'I hate divorce', says God, 'and covering one's garment with violence, so ... be faithful.'

If a couple is caught in the act of adultery, it should be both of them, not just the woman, facing the horrific prospect of execution by public stoning. So when (John 8) Jesus is presented with the woman accused of adultery (some apocryphal Gospel accounts have her only accused, not caught, and her co-respondent is nowhere in sight) it isn't just a moral point when he demands that the sinless casts the first stone; the lynch mob is itself in violation of the law.

Even those famous instructions to be submissive may not be exactly what they've often been made out to be. It's a recurring theme in Paul's letters that the proper Christian attitude to other people is to 'regard others more highly than yourself' (Phil. 2.3), which he applies to relationships as casual as acquaintances in Church, or to members of different religious traditions. So naturally there will be similar standards expected between husbands and wives. Ephesians 5 makes it clear that submission is mutual, not one sided; and Peter, whatever (on earth!) he was thinking of when he made those remarks about unfair beatings, lists in 1 Peter 3 what constitutes a healthy intimate relationship: shared purpose, mutual support, sympathy, love, tenderness and humility.

Looking critically and thoughtfully at the Bible, there are even some case studies that turn out to be textbook examples of attitudes to violence against women, and how, or how not, to deal with it.

In Judges 19, there is the tale of what happens to a woman who marries a Levite, and becomes so unhappy that she runs away. The woman's father also appears to be abusive, drunkenly colluding with the Levite when he arrives to take her back. On the return journey the couple are offered hospitality in a strange town, where, as with Lot's visitors at Sodom, a mob gathers outside and demands that the male guest is presented for homosexual abuse. The charming host offers the mob his virgin daughter instead. They decline, so the Levite literally throws the concubine into the street for them, where she is subjected all night to horrific gang rape, and left unconscious on the doorstep. When the Levite trips over her body in the morning, he actually orders her to get up. Since she doesn't reply, he dumps her on his donkey and goes home. Finding her dead on arrival, he dismembers her body and sends a piece to each of the 12 tribes of Israel.

The story bears all the appalling hallmarks of relationship violence that modern psychology and sociology can teach us. The woman goes from one abusive situation to another, almost

Crucible is published quarterly by Hymns Ancient & Modern Ltd.
Registered Charity No. 270060

It is edited by John Atherton, in collaboration with the
Church of England's Division of Mission and Public Affairs;
the William Temple Foundation and the Department of
Theology and Religious Studies, Chester University.

Correspondence and articles
Correspondence and articles for submission should be sent to John
Atherton, 102 Fairview Drive, Adlington, Chorley, Lancs, PR6 9ST:
john.atherton@talktalk.net. Articles should be of about 3000 words.
Books for review to should be sent to Dr Elizabeth Phillips,
Westcott House, Jesus Lane, Cambridge CB5 8BP.

Subscriptions
(for four copies): individual rate £20; institutions £27;
international (includes airmail) £38. Single copies cost £6.
All prices included postage and packing. Cheques should
be made payable to Crucible, and sent to: Crucible subscriptions,
Subscription Manager, 13a Hellesdon Park Road, Norwich NR6 5DR.

Tel: 01603 785 910   Fax: 01603 624483.
crucible@hymnsam.co.uk

Direct Debit forms available from the same address

ISSN 0011-2100
ISBN 9780334053774

Printed by Blackwell Print & Web Communication,
Charles Street, Great Yarmouth, Norfolk, NR30 3LA

Contents

socialized into thinking this is normal. When she manages to escape, the abuser goes to fetch her back. He has the knack of finding like-minded company for himself, and shows nothing but contempt for the victim. And it's after the attempt to leave that the woman is killed, demonstrating how dangerous this course of action can be.

There is no repentance, no restitution, no rescue, not even a show of disapproval. To our shame, it's a story whose grisly details, far from being an episode confined to the dustbin of history, are still being played out in accounts of gang rape in India, in Central Africa, and in the grooming, abuse and handing around for sex of young girls in the care system here in the UK. The ghastly tearing apart of a woman's body and its distribution throughout the tribes of Israel serves as a tragic metaphor of how widespread and revolting violence against women is.

The horror of the tragic story of Jephthah's daughter (Judges 11) is compounded by the way it has been presented, for most of Christian history, as a cautionary tale against making a rash promise, or even as the epitome of daughterly devotion, rather than as a cold-blooded example of cruelty. Jephthah, a formerly despised thug- turned-military-leader whose back-story may help explain though not excuse his appalling behaviour, makes a cynical bargain with God. He promises to sacrifice the first living thing he sees coming out of his house, if God lets him win the battle. When his darling only daughter comes skipping along, playing her tambourine and singing of daddy's victory, he regretfully enacts his vow. She persuades him to let her to spend a few weeks in the hills with her friends first, mourning her lost womanhood; and the tale ends by describing how every year, the teenage girls of Israel withdraw into the countryside to commemorate her fate.

Again, the typical hallmarks of abuse are there. Jephthah learns no compassion and chooses to show none. Born of a married man's casual affair, his paternal role model was cynical and distant, with a selfish attitude to women – so that abuse is again perpetrated through the generations. Jephthah takes no responsibility for committing murder, plays for sympathy, and even claims he was driven to it by his victim, blaming her for being first out of the house to greet him: 'You have broken my heart!'

Perhaps most famously, there is the story of the rape of King David's daughter Tamar, by her half-brother Amnon, proving that domestic abuse can happen in any class of society. Yet again, a grimly familiar pattern emerges (2 Sam. 13.1–22). Two men, Amnon and Jonadab, conspire to perpetrate the offence. Careful planning and deceit is involved, and Amnon's status ensures that the servant he drags into the cover-up won't dare speak out. Afterwards, Amnon projects his feelings of revulsion onto his victim. Older brother Absalom tumbles to what has happened and offers Tamar sanctuary in his house, but ham-fistedly advises her 'not to take it to heart', and not to report the rape, as it will bring shame on the family. The mighty King David does nothing, and the cover-up results in a massive feud ending in more murder. Tamar never recovers, dying tragically young, the Bible tells us, lonely and desolate. At the very end of the chapter, we learn that Absalom went on to have four children, including a beautiful daughter called Tamar. After his tragic mishandling of events, it seems Absalom finally determined that the story should be brought into the open; and after all the anonymous victims, at least Tamar's name is known and remembered.

And thankfully, there are some contrasting and positive examples in the Bible of how to deal with vulnerable women.

Instead of Jephthah's daughter, dying on the brink of womanhood at the hand of her father, we have Jairus, calling Jesus to heal the daughter who falls sick at a similar age. Instead of making a dead girl, the ultimate passive woman!, an example of dutiful daughterhood, Jesus calls her to 'Rise up' and embrace the future (Luke 8.54).

The Levite's concubine, fleeing an abusive marriage, never has the chance to speak for herself, and is tortured to death, with no one held to account. Faced with a woman accused of adultery, Jesus publically shames the men about to stone her, then asks the woman if she feels safe from her torturers – 'Does anyone here condemn you?' (John 8.10) – before putting the future into her hands.

Those who know about Tamar's rape say nothing and persuade her to keep quiet for fear of scandal. When the Samaritan woman at the well is ostracized because she has been married five times, Jesus recognizes everything there is to know about her situation. Jesus not only understands her but trusts her, and restores her confidence to the extent that she becomes an influential woman in her society, telling everyone about the Good News of the Messiah.

Crucible January 2015

Instead of colluding with the abuse, disbelieving the victims, blaming them, or at best trying to cover it up, we see the problem confronted, victims listened to and trusted, perpetrators shamed, and women restored to the status not of submissive wives, but of independent people with choices about their lives and with influence on society.

The Bible is an ancient text which reflects some attitudes and behaviours we now find abhorrent. We reap the legacy of some of these attitudes today, as the following articles testify. But at the very least, the stark horror of their inclusion in our scriptures shows us that God knows exactly what might be going on behind closed doors, that atrocities are taken on and experienced even by God, and that we need to not only see the face of God in the victim but learn how to bring truth, justice and new life into being.

Carol Wardman is Bishops' Adviser for Church and Society, Church in Wales.

Encounters of a Parish Priest

PEGGY JACKSON

This article is essentially anecdotal, an account of some experiences of one Anglican parish priest over two or three decades and various encounters with the issues of violence against women. These were decades, during which the face of the Church of England changed dramatically in relation to women. They were also decades when change was happening in the justice system and to many of the social norms of British society. The lid was being lifted on domestic abuse in its variety of forms and matters exposed which had previously been protected behind the solid screen of family issues or household privacy. The biggest change in society was that victims began to find a voice and to be believed. And since the majority of victims were women, it was violence against women that was now being exposed in ways which shocked and then unsettled, almost every one of the old institutions. Germaine Greer's *The Female Eunuch* had been published in 1970; the first women's refuge opened in Chiswick in 1971; the first Rape Crisis Centre opened in 1973; and to the surprise of many, a large proportion of the first clients who sought help were older women, needing to disclose and work through historic experiences of rape and abuse.

As a parish priest, my first encounter with violence against women arose through a pastoral counselling relationship. A parishioner in her fifties sought help with repeated bouts of depression, and, in the course of lengthy conversations, began to recover her memory of sexual abuse as a child, which had gone on systematically from the time she was four until she was around 15. We were meeting in the early 1990s, when some high-profile public enquiries were beginning to bring the sexual abuse of children to public attention, and victims were feeling, for the first time, that they could come forward, and expect to be believed. Like so many others, she had been disbelieved and silenced as a young child, when trying to tell a Sunday school teacher what was happening; in her teenage years, she was silenced by a combination of shame, threats and fear, because by then she had been made complicit in the ongoing abuse of other children, younger than herself. By the time she reached adulthood, she had effectively suppressed all these memories. As a young wife and mother, she had begun to suffer from depression, which led her into the hands of ignorant medical authorities, and effectively new forms of abuse. She had a spell of addiction to anti-depressants, was hospitalized by mental health professionals, and subjected to clumsy sex advice from a dapperly-dressed psychiatrist sitting behind his professional desk, while he and her husband discussed what they perceived as her problem, but without any idea of her actual story.

What brought her to me to begin to uncover this story was not just greater awareness growing in the public sphere, but also the fact that, for the first time, the local Anglican parish had provided a woman to minister with authority in that congregation. Women deacons from 1987, and priests from 1994, were beginning to take pastoral charge of congregations and changing the visible face of the Church of England, changing the way in which the Church was seen to regard women. For the first time this gave out a message that women's voices could be of value because they were women, and women's experience of the world was essential to set alongside men's for a full understanding of what it is to be a human being. It seems extraordinary to say this now but only 30 years ago, those assumptions were not automatic.

At the same time, what enabled me to hear and believe what she was telling me, was not the traditional sources of church pastoral guidance but a new generation of feminist theology and feminist liturgies which were being written and made available to women ministers such as myself, who were looking urgently for support and resources to improve our insight and meet the demands of our new ministries. Theology, prayers and liturgical material being produced by groups such as Women in Theology (founded in the early 1980s) and the St Hilda Community, and contributors to the Ecumenical Decade of Churches in Solidarity with Women (designated by the World Council of Churches, 1988–98), did begin to offer a narrative on which I could draw and within which I could set my parishioner's individual experience, and work with her, to come through to a newer more adult way of understanding. From there, she was able in time to make adult choices which were able to begin to reframe her life. Not only her, but in the course of the next eight years in that parish, I became aware of five different women members of that congregation (which only totalled 50), who had also suffered domestic abuse which had coloured the whole outlook of their lives.

At one point, I had asked diocesan resource officers and other senior women colleagues for help and advice in relation to my continuing care for this parishioner. I was disconcerted by finding they had nothing to offer. Indeed one preferred to cast doubt on the likely veracity of the story itself. The only people who acknowledged their experience of such stories were those working in the traditional area of healing ministries. But not surprisingly, since ordained women had not been around for very long, these areas were still predominantly being led by male priests, and they tended to work with quite traditional models of health and wholeness which were actually at risk of exacerbating the very issues my parishioner was already trying to redefine. At one point, I became very concerned on my own behalf as to why I seemed to have attracted this story and its disclosures when other ministers had not, a concern which sent me scurrying off to seek some years of personal counselling in order to unravel some elements of my own past. Through this, I discovered various common threads of mid-life work, some of which must be common to all adults, but other parts of which seem particular to women because of the ways in which women have been assigned their roles and status within a largely patriarchal society.

Perhaps it is a sign of the way in which ordained women were still in the early stages of negotiating their roles in the Church at this time, but all of that process by which I sought and found help for myself and my ministry was done outside the formal channels of church and clergy training programmes (apart from a limited grant for some personal counselling sessions). Women in ministry in the Church, it seems, just like women in society and in the world, were having to search out their own means of making sense of their experience, and work out their own paths towards healing. But being able to share their journeys, and bring a sacramental dimension into that process, meant that women survivors of violence and abuse began to find in the Church a new understanding and validation of their experience from the inside. Here was the possibility of real transformation, both for those women, and for the Church which was able now to embrace and incorporate a much wider perception of the world's reality.

Soon after my parishioner began to uncover her own story, she responded to an advertisement in the diocesan newspaper for anyone who had suffered abuse in a church context to make contact. Although thus described, the convenor was happy to broaden the criteria for inclusion, and I accompanied my parishioner to a first meeting of what was to become a small ongoing self-help group. It met monthly, to support the members as they worked through various aspects of their individual journeys towards healing, and, coming from a wide area but using our church rooms, they also asked me to stay on as a safe listener to help the group do its work. The convenor herself was a survivor of years of childhood abuse from an older sibling, who went on to a high profile role within the Church, but who had never been confronted. Several had stories of unhelpful interventions by church healing ministries that had exacerbated their problems. One (who came occasionally to me for additional one-to-one listening sessions) had experienced years of systematic satanic abuse; some strands of this seemed apparently to be ongoing into her adult life, even while she was simultaneously bringing up her own young family and apparently presenting herself to the world as a model of churchgoing probity.

A question for me, in all this, was what sort of ministry I should be offering to this group, and how that related to more traditional church categories of healing, reconciliation or liberation. In the absence of anything available through church clerical channels, I sought out helpful supervision from a professional psychotherapist friend, and from time to time, it was appropriate to offer and carry through a sacramental ministry with individuals. But in retrospect, it seems that the overriding sacramental task was, as a priest of the Church, to listen, and in that listening for the Church to hear, perhaps for the first time, the truths of these of its members which they had never before dared to reveal. These were confessions, not of personal sin requiring a ministry of reconciliation, but of victimhood which required Christ-centred healing by a ministry of validation and affirmation.

At the same time, the Church itself, in response to shocking public revelations of abuse, was having in the 1990s to take great

Crucible January 2015

steps to examine its own policies and practice. The self-help group members were heartened to be invited to contribute, as the first diocesan child protection policies and procedures were being drafted. They were also consulted, when the first pastoral guidelines were prepared in the diocese for clergy women and men working together, and for good practice for clergy in pastoral situations where personal boundaries were particularly important. This was because it was recognized that survivors of abuse in childhood were often particularly vulnerable to violence or controlling behaviours, long after they had grown into adulthood. Clergy and parishes needed to be aware of the origins of such inculcated patterns of behaviour, as well as examining and addressing their own often unchallenged habits. The group also found strength in contacts shared with the more public organization Christian Survivors of Sexual Abuse, which had been established by Margaret Kennedy in 1989, with a particular focus on victims of abuses committed by the clergy.

In 1998 I moved to a large suburban parish in southwest London, and found opportunity there to play a role, on behalf of the Church, in liaising with the local authority and other agencies. The initiative was clearly coming at this time from secular authorities. A Conference on Domestic Violence was convened by the office of the Mayor of London. It brought together representatives from all the major faith communities, and the report arising from the day became a key document in developing and funding local initiatives to address domestic abuse issues on a wider scale. My local borough established a new co-ordinator post, funded by Victim Support, to raise awareness generally and work for active social change. The post was supported by a borough-wide Domestic Violence Forum, which brought together the statutory agencies (police, magistrates, social services etc.) with a range of charities and churches engaged in an agenda for change. This was possibly the first time that I experienced the Church's ability to play a significant role, and be regarded as contributing to the solution to these issues, instead of being stereotyped and assumed to be a major part of the problem.

A personal breakthrough came for me in the Forum when, during a discussion about how to arrange a suitable fundraising and awareness event (something more than just a roadshow with stalls), I was able to suggest holding a carol service. It was no easy task to persuade the coordinator that such an event could deliver what the Forum wanted. Her reluctance was very evident. But in the end, because we could offer the church as a very flexible space, able to include exhibition space alongside the gathering area and room for refreshments afterwards as well as a team of willing volunteers to help, she relented. We sang carols, devised prayers and gave space for courageous personal testimony from survivors as well as receiving performances by professional guest singers. It went very well, achieving all that we had hoped. We were even able to offer a safe opportunity for some women who were living in one of the local refuges to attend. And, being reminded that women and children found it particularly hard to be there, even for their own safety, over Christmas, because they were completely cut off from loved ones and their wider families, we were able to channel some extra Christmas gifts from the churches that year to be shared by families in the refuge. In the relief and general appreciation which followed, the coordinator disclosed to me the reason for her initial reluctance to have any such event linked with the Church: when she was nine years old, she had witnessed the murder of her mother by her father, and then had experienced the caring ministry of the Christian Church in the shape of their local pastor, whose main energy had been directed towards mounting the strongest possible defence of her father. In the circumstances I was amazed at the generosity and courage she had shown in allowing a different face of the Church the opportunity to recover some of its integrity in living and acting on the gospel we preach.

Subsequently, annual carol services followed, one of the most memorable of which included as guest speaker Erin Pizzey, the founder of the first ever women's refuge in Chiswick. She reminded us powerfully of the need to prioritize care for the children in situations of domestic violence, who, even though they may not always be the direct targets of acts of violence, often suffer the long-term consequences and damage arising from it. She told of the early days of their house in Chiswick, where even as she continued to provide a haven for desperate women, who were quite literally arriving on the doorstep, she was being denounced from the pulpit of her local Anglican church for undermining family life. The only thing that kept her going through those days, she said, was her faith.

That Domestic Violence Forum was a place where it felt

Crucible January 2015

entirely hopeful that the Church could take its place, among and alongside other agencies, building trust between professionals, representatives and volunteers and recognizing the complementary roles that each could play in the wider agenda to raise public awareness and challenge the culture of wilful blindness towards violence suffered by women. At the same time, our diocese took the opportunity to sponsor an initiative towards all parishes, urging them to discuss and heighten awareness of the issues of domestic abuse. A Charter was published for discussion by PCCs. This could then be posted up in churches as a visible sign that the Church had begun to understand and take seriously the experience of all victims of domestic violence. It promised the church building, and congregation, as a place of safety where people would be believed and helped in appropriate ways. It was accompanied by a series of training evenings for congregation members, as well as clergy and PCC representatives, where the facts of domestic violence in our society were communicated, and people helped to learn how to ask sensitive questions in a way which was also prepared to hear and believe, and respond appropriately, to the answers.

Later on, also through contact made in the Forum, I was privileged to be asked by one of the refuge houses to lead some prayers in the house for healing and safety. These were to be accessible for women of several different faiths who were living there, but who had agreed to seek help because of the particularly troubled concerns of one of their number. Through the visit, and talking with her in her room, it became apparent that since her room was situated right beside the main front door of the house through which women came, with all their immediate fears and anxieties when they first arrived, she seemed in some sense to be mediating the troubles contained within the house as a whole, as, literally they passed her door on a daily basis. The occasion was, however, a gift of recognition to the church that we could be seen to have something of value to offer to women who up to then had been given little reason to expect any help from their established religious institutions.

Survivors of domestic abuse will say, again and again, that the one thing which begins to change their situation and opens the door to transformation and future safety, is their being believed. When victims began to be believed by the major social institutions, doctors, schools, police, social services etc., then relief could be found for individuals, and the systemic violence of our society towards women could begin to be named and challenged. We still have a long way to go for this process to be complete, and the churches have, for most of this journey, been as much a part of the problem as they have the solution. It is no mere coincidence that these same decades have been ones of struggle within the Anglican Church towards equality between women and men in relation to ordination and authority within the Church. It has been no less than a struggle for recognition of the full humanity of women, on the basis of which women could be deemed capable of receiving the grace of ordination, and representing at the altar what it is to stand before God as a fully human being. How could our churches have ever been capable of hearing and believing the testimony of women suffering the hidden abuses of domestic violence, while they were unable to acknowledge or give credence to the authority and witness of women in their midst who were speaking of vocations to ordination and asking for that to be tested in public. It is only as the Church has begun to realize and value the experience of women, as necessary for a full understanding of the world and human society, that it has also begun to hear, and therefore be able to respond, to women's testimony about the reality of their lives. Perhaps it has taken the ordination of women, and placing women clergy into positions of public trust and authority alongside their male colleagues, to enable the Church regain some of that trust in society that it was once able to take for granted. Certainly, its credibility among women who have suffered domestic violence will continue for a long time to depend upon its ability to listen, and take seriously, the experience of all women who look to their faith for understanding and hope.

Peggy Jackson is Archdeacon of Llandaff.

Dealing with Domestic Violence

A Police Perspective

SIMON PRINCE

Violence against women takes on many guises. It could be domestic abuse as is evident in the televised soap operas, it may be the sexual harassment of a female student, or it could be the stalking of a woman by her ex-husband. Police officers are trained to look for signs, not just of physical abuse but also of sexual and emotional abuse, signs of those who dictate the family finances to elicit control and those that assert who a woman is allowed to speak to or what she is allowed to wear. Some women may not even be aware that they are being subjected to abuse, but they will find themselves in situations where all control has been taken from them. Some women will recognize their situation is wrong and be able to walk away, others may be unable to escape the relationship due to the fear of violence. A woman is killed on average every two days in England and Wales: approximately half of these women are killed by their current or former partners. These are figures which are slowly decreasing but clearly require continued focus.

A woman being subjected to violence and abuse is, and unfortunately always has been, part of every officer's daily duties. Whilst modern day attitudes have undergone a seismic shift from those that were previously commonplace, there still exists an aura of shame. Sadly, this shame most often lies, wrongly, with the victims, who are encouraged by perpetrators to see themselves as being somehow responsible for the abuse. This perception is a clear barrier to confiding in others about the abuse, allowing it to continue unchecked. Mistrust of the criminal justice system is a further hurdle, as previous experiences of the process, from the initial police response through to the court room, found it to be just that for some women – a process. Those subjected to violence have found themselves answering questions to police officers and medical professionals; they may have been physically photographed and examined and then asked to attend court, facing questions about their personal relationship. Any one of those experiences would cause a normal person to feel deeply anxious and yet victims have been asked to do all of these things at a time when they will be feeling emotionally and physically fragile. It is little wonder that women have often withdrawn from criminal proceedings; it is the only decision left that they have control over.

Within Dyfed-Powys Police we have recognized the need to change how we work with victims of domestic violence if we are to gain their trust and ensure the perpetrator is brought to justice. We have implemented schemes that put the control back into the hands of women, and the police service nationally has dedicated a great deal of time and effort over recent years to professionalize the way violence against women is dealt with. Such changes have been formed in conjunction with statutory partners in the criminal justice system, local authorities and third-sector organizations.

Response officers called to a report of violence or domestic abuse are often faced with a fast moving scenario and have very little time to establish a rapport with the victim. Dyfed-Powys Police have addressed this by introducing Operation Baltic, an enhanced response to incidents of domestic violence. A trial period initially ran over the high-risk Christmas period of 2013, and this was followed by similar deployments during the Six Nations Rugby Tour and the Football World Cup weekends. Operation Baltic provides a dedicated and highly-skilled domestic violence officer teamed with a response officer utilizing a fast response car. They will become the first response to any domestic incident reported to the police. We've taken the domestic violence abuse officers out of the office and made them available to work directly with the victim from the start, allowing us to gather the best evidence and providing the answers and reassurance needed at that very early stage.

Working alongside our domestic violence abuse officers are Independent Domestic Violence Advisors (IDVAs). As the name suggests, the advisors are independent from the police and all other agencies and provide ongoing emotional support to victims at high risk of continued abuse. If a perpetrator, possibly the sole earner, is subjected by the police to conditions banning him from contacting the victim, a woman may find herself in a different but equally difficult position. The advisors are available to many women providing and signposting practical support and advice from childcare and travel arrangements through to housing and financial arrangements. This level of support is essential if women are to feel confident that they can continue with criminal proceedings without their home life grinding to a halt in the background. Investment in the provision of independent advisors for Dyfed-Powys has more than doubled in the last few months as the recognition of their positive outcomes for victims has been acknowledged, and we strive to provide further support within our communities.

Domestic Violence Protection Notices (DVPNs) have been introduced across the country as a further control measure for those perpetrators who seek to return, and continue the abuse of a partner. The DVPN can be issued by the police, endorsed and continued by the magistrate's court, in the form of a court order, providing emergency short-term protective measures for a woman whilst allowing the numerous agencies available to work in a coordinated approach to support her. This tool can be utilized to place the offender under certain conditions such as to prevent them returning to the home address or making contact with their partner. This can completely remove the need for women and children to leave their home at short notice for their own protection. Formerly this would have presented another barrier to women proceeding with a criminal prosecution.

The ongoing support for women facing domestic abuse comes from many different areas, therefore it is essential to coordinate these efforts. The police, nationally, engage in the Multi-Agency Risk Assessment Conference (MARAC) process for high-risk and repeat domestic abuse cases and those where a serial perpetrator is identified. This process regularly brings together the various support agencies to share information, formulate ideas and strategically plan how best to support the woman moving forward. The issues discussed may range from housing and employment through to the police investigation and the woman's protection from harassment by an ex-partner.

As an organization we are designing an information sharing hub, a central location to co-locate victim services for Dyfed-

Crucible January 2015

Powys such as the independent domestic violence advisors, along with partners such as social services and housing associations. Encouraging the co-location of services with shared IT databases will ensure that information sharing between agencies becomes a natural flow that occurs as it becomes known rather than waiting for the next meeting. Cases will no longer fall through the gaps, serial perpetrators can be stopped earlier, and women can be offered better coordinated support.

Information sharing doesn't just exist for the agencies dealing with violence against women. The introduction of schemes such as Clare's Law are providing relevant and timely information for the women at the heart of this matter. The scheme is designed to shift the decision making and control back to the woman. It allows women or their family members, to request information on partners they believe may have a history of domestic abuse. As a police service, we are now enabled to inform that person if their partner has a history of domestic abuse, thus allowing them to make their own informed decisions at an early juncture before they become subject to any attacks.

Changes in legislation have also brought about specific domestic violence court hearings for dealing with domestic abuse cases. The magistrates undergo a higher level of training in the subject to ensure they fully understand the risks, Crown prosecutors use expedited case working to ensure cases are heard quicker, and prosecutions can be brought without the victim of the abuse being required to give evidence in court. All of these changes have allowed criminal proceedings to become quicker and more streamlined, reducing the time an offender spends on bail but also the time spent by the victim worrying about the case.

Dyfed-Powys police is also working with the individuals responsible for violence against women; we are using the Domestic Abuse, Stalking and Harassment (DASH) Risk Assessment to help identify at the scene of an incident, not just were the victim has been repeatedly targeted, but alternatively where the offender has repeatedly targeted partners. Work has recently been undertaken with these serial perpetrators of domestic abuse to help them to understand their behaviour and the effects it has on victims and the others affected by their actions, such as children, with the intention of preventing them from reoffending.

Looking to the future; what should we be expecting? The

Crucible January 2015

police service has made great strides in treating the symptoms of domestic abuse and violence against women, and we have put measures in place to prevent offending, to identify and support women subjected to violence and to increase the prosecution of offenders. But is there a far greater role to be played by society in treating the cause of domestic violence?

Recent research by the Nation Union of Students (NUS) showed that 50 per cent of study participants, both male and female, experienced 'prevailing sexism, "laddism" and a culture of harassment' at their universities. Given the increasing cultural intolerance to violence against women, it is odd to see such a trend emerging. This behaviour may be viewed as alcohol-fuelled high jinx, but how will this present itself in the future? Will these same individuals still believe in 15 years' time that it is acceptable to emotionally abuse their partners, name call and sexually assault women, as they see fit? Will these experiences cause young women to become conditioned in the belief that is it normal to be treated in such a way by others? There is a clear case for further research into this type of behaviour, establishing the root cause of such beliefs. Consideration is needed around how to deal with these issues across all partner agencies from schools and GP surgeries to social services and the police.

There is still work to be done but in summary, keeping women involved, informed and giving them back the control of their situation is paramount if we are to maintain our drive against domestic abuse. However, there will always be opportunities for every person in society to do more and change the attitude towards domestic abuse.

Simon Prince is Chief Constable for Dyfed-Powys Police and National Police Lead for Chaplaincy.

In Churches Too

Violence against Women and What Action Churches Can Take

MANDY MARSHALL

Women aged 15–44 are more at risk from rape and domestic violence than from cancer, car accidents, war and malaria (United Nations a).

Facing reality

Every year, millions of women and girls worldwide suffer violence. Something that is wholly and utterly preventable. This violence can take many forms such as domestic violence, rape, sexual violence, trafficking, female genital mutilation, child brides and dowry-related killing (this is not an exclusive list) (United Nations a). In some countries up to 70 per cent of women have experienced physical and/or sexual violence in their lifetime from an intimate partner (United Nations b).

The size of those statistics are shocking and overwhelming. It can lead to a paralysis in action as the realization of the depth and breadth of the issue of violence against women globally hits home. Indeed reflecting that each statistic represents an individual made in the image of God, the reality is devastating. Yet it is a truth that must be faced if violence against women is to be ended.

The United Nations defines violence against women as 'violence that results in, or is likely to result in, physical, sexual or psychological harm or suffering to women, including threats of such acts, coercion, arbitrary deprivations of liberty, whether occurring in public or private life' (United Nations c).

Sexual violence affects an estimated one in five women globally. The impact and consequences of an intimate violation of the body can result in extensive physical and psychological trauma, along with unwanted pregnancies. Sexual violence in conflict has been long recognized as a tactic of war. In the Democratic Republic of

Congo (DRC) an average of 36 women and girls are raped every day. It is estimated that 200,000 women have been raped in the DRC since the conflict began. During the genocide in Rwanda in 1994 it is estimated that between 250,000 and 500,000 women were raped. Female Genital Mutilation (FGM) affects between 100 and 140 million girls worldwide with another 3,000,000 girls estimated to be at risk of FGM (United Nations a).

As no respecter of age, culture, ethnicity or wealth, violence against women has its foundations in gender inequality and discrimination against women. At its heart is the abuse of power and control over another individual. This was made evident in the UK when in 2013 the TV chef Nigella Lawson was photographed being abused by her then husband. Something she described as intimate terrorism. As a famous, wealthy, and much loved celebrity chef, it came as a surprise to many that she was being abused by her husband. It cut across the myth that wealth is a protector from violence. It is not.

The UK Home Office recently updated and expanded the definition of domestic violence which is now defined as 'any incident or pattern of incidents of controlling, coercive or threatening behaviour, violence or abuse between those aged 16 or over who have been intimate partners or family members regardless of gender or sexuality. This can encompass but is not limited to, the following types of abuse: psychological, physical, sexual, financial, emotional.' (Home Office) The inclusion of pattern of incidents reflects the lived reality of many victims of domestic abuse, noting that whilst physical violence may be the trigger in reporting there is often a build-up and pattern of abuse beforehand. The inclusion of financial abuse also may challenge thinking about what abuse is. For example, a woman may not have access or control over the household income and is coerced or forced into sex by the husband and partner simply to obtain the housekeeping money.

The levels of domestic abuse in the UK are significant. According to the UK Office of National Statistics: '30.0 per cent of women and 16.3 per cent of men had experienced any domestic abuse since the age of 16, equivalent to an estimated 4.9 million female victims of domestic abuse and 2.7 million male victims.' (ONS a) Looking at the levels of sexual assault the ONS states that 'many more women than men experienced some form of sexual

24

assault (including attempts) in the last year: three per cent of women compared with 0.3 per cent of men' (ONS b). The statistics go on to dispel the myth of stranger rape by noting that 'around 90 per cent of victims of the most serious sexual offences in the previous year knew the perpetrator' (ONS c).

The impact and consequences of violence on victims and survivors can be devastating and lifelong. Women may suffer the horrific consequences of abuse such as broken bones, lifelong health issues, diminished roles in public and private life, loss of economic earning power, loss of relationships with friends and family, loss of self-confidence and psychological trauma. In the worst cases violence against women results in the loss of life itself. Women's Aid report that 'on average two women a week are killed by a violent partner or ex-partner' (Women's Aid 2005). The levels of these statistics need to move us into action.

In churches too

With 4.9 million female victims of domestic abuse in England and Wales alone we cannot ignore the reality that this will mean that women who have experienced domestic abuse will be in churches too. Many through shame, stigma or the lack of a safe place to disclose that abuse, will remain and suffer in silence in our churches. Charlotte's (a pseudonym) story highlights this issue.

Charlotte was a young Christian woman, when she ended up in a relationship with a man named Craig, who chose to abuse her for six years. What started off as seemingly romantic gestures, such as the need to always be close to Charlotte, gradually escalated into manipulative and controlling behaviour. This included limiting the communication she was allowed with her family and friends and insisting she had her phone on her at all times, so that he could always contact her.

Craig's desire to control Charlotte and their relationship got worse, until he was both emotionally and physically abusing her. During one moment of overwhelming anger, he hit her over the back of the head, then profusely apologized and promised it would never happen again. But, it did. In fact, the physical abuse, including rape, became so frequent and extreme that when Charlotte finally summed up the courage and will to leave Craig, she had to undergo five months of intense physiotherapy to get her limbs working properly again, as well as several months of counselling for post-traumatic stress disorder.

The sad and shocking truth is that Charlotte's case is by no means rare. However, there is a common view that domestic abuse only occurs in certain social groups and to certain kinds of women, perhaps those who are poor and uneducated , and most definitely not to Christians! Recalling her experiences Charlotte said: 'There was no actual hostility at the church, but I just felt that it was too much to try to talk about the abuse, as I really felt that nobody would understand but would be wanting to know details or would think that I was exaggerating the severity.'

Charlotte's story brings a challenge to churches about how safe space is being advertised and provided for victims and survivors of abuse to get the help and support needed. Not that churches are expected to be experts but rather that churches need to be linked in locally to the professional services available, so that referrals can be made or information provided so that victims or survivors of abuse can access that professional support.

Statistics for the levels of violence against women happening in our churches are difficult to find and rare. *Restored* (Restored a) is hoping to conduct such a survey in association with a university in the near future. Research data which is available was produced by the Methodist Church in 2002. This survey found that 17 per cent of respondents had experienced domestic violence, 13 per cent had experienced domestic violence several times, 54 per cent said they had experienced domestic violence for five years of more and that the main perpetrators of domestic violence were husbands and partners (Methodist Report 2002). More recently the Evangelical Alliance stated in its *How's the Family* report in 2012 that ten per cent of women experienced physical abuse, and seven per cent of men admitted perpetrating physical abuse (Evangelical Alliance 2012).

Christian survivors of abuse give varied stories of how churches have addressed the issue of domestic abuse when it has been disclosed. With a diverse and varied culture that operates in churches in the UK, the response has differed generally from church to church. Some survivors reported that their church had been helpful and supportive. Yet many that *Restored* listened to faced silence, unhelpful responses, collusion with the perpetrator of the violence, and in some cases, Scripture being used to coerce survivors to stay or return to abusive husbands and partners (Archbishop 2014). At best this is naive, at worst this is lethal.

Myths

Often the response from churches reflects some of the myths around abuse. The most common being 'why doesn't she just leave?', as if leaving a relationship was simple. In fact in the UK a woman is most at risk of death at the point of or just after leaving a relationship. It can be a very dangerous time as the perpetrator loses power and control over the victim. The question that should be asked is 'why doesn't he stop?'.

Another myth is that a perpetrator abuses his partner due to anger issues, alcohol or job loss. This plays into the myth that abuse happens because of something else, an external force, which the perpetrator has no control over. In fact abuse is a choice. Stating that it's something external allows the perpetrator to deflect responsibility for their attitudes and actions.

Churches can add another dimension to the myths of abuse. The combination of the use, misuse and misunderstanding of Scripture can provide a toxic environment for abuse to continue and a victim to stay longer when it's not safe to do so. This combination can look like 'if I only pray more, submit more, God can transform anyone, my husband is my head, and I should obey him, divorce is wrong', rather than taking Jesus as an example of how to operate in relationship with one another.

There is a need for churches to be clear that violence against women is wrong and must stop. When our church culture silences, is complicit, or can lead to death, then our church culture has to change. We need to break the silence and speak out about abuse.

There is a need to re-emphasize that all violence against women is wrong and must stop, that Scripture cannot be used to justify violence, that the church has an answer and can be part of the solution, that men and women can work together to end violence against women and that the time to act is now.

What can churches do?

The first action churches can take is to acknowledge the reality of the statistics and recognize that domestic abuse happens in churches too. This can then lead into discussions and solutions offered by churches depending on their own context and resources. The Revd Graeme Skinner of St. Mary's Church, Upton has devoted whole services to the issue of abuse and has produced a liturgy (Restored b). In a church context it can be key to undo the mixed messages of the toxic theology combination that can create an enabling environment for abuse to occur. Using theology and sermons to challenge abuse can be incredibly helpful to a victim, a survivor, and also challenge perpetrators of abuse who may well be sitting in the congregation. Being clear that all violence against women is wrong and must stop breaks the myth that abuse can't happen in churches as well as beginning to address wrongly applied theology.

Church leaders, and particularly pastoral care officers, may find attending a basic awareness training on domestic abuse, what it is and how to address it, useful in the course of their work. Where there are already safeguarding officers and procedures, a domestic violence referral line can be added in so that women who are abused know who they can contact in church and know that they will be listened to in safety. *Restored* offers a free pack for churches on ending domestic abuse (Restored b) alongside basic awareness training. Churches Together in Cumbria have had their own domestic abuse awareness training programme linked with the local professional services. There is a lot churches can choose to do when it becomes a priority.

A charter for churches is another action that can be taken, with the charter prominently displayed or distributed in the church (Restored b). This signifies that the church is aware of the issue of domestic abuse and is prepared to take action. For victims and survivors coming into the church it signals that the church is a safe place, and for perpetrators that they need to stop.

It is important that churches, where possible and feasible, link into local professional services available. Supporting local refuges and safe houses, within a set of agreed boundaries and guidelines, can be a real support to survivors of abuse when they could be otherwise isolated and alone. Some churches have provided so called pamper packs for refuges, noting that often women have left home with very little clothing or essentials.

Engaging men

Thankfully there are many men who choose not to abuse: many men are good fathers, husbands, or partners. Sometimes though these men do not speak up or challenge violence and abuse when it is seen or heard. The quote from Edmund Burke becomes so obvious here: 'The only thing necessary for the triumph of evil is for good men to do nothing.' There are several campaigns that have recently come to the fore that highlight the importance of engaging good men in the response to violence against women. Originating from the White Ribbon Campaign in Canada, First Man Standing encourages Christian men to respect all women, challenge other men's attitudes and actions towards women and join in the cause with women to end violence against them (Restored c). The UN recently relaunched its 'He for She' (UN d), a solidarity movement for gender equality, which includes ending violence against women.

Whilst there are many constructive aspects of these campaigns, there is a need to ensure that there is positive action as a result, that men do not use it as an opportunity to take up power over women in a new or different sphere, thus contributing to abuse. It is important that the campaigns have a reference group of women that can contribute and advise on courses of action, remembering that at the heart of violence is the abuse of power and control. It is important that women and men work together to bring violence against women to an end. After all, if violence against women is to stop, then it is the attitudes and actions of men that have to change.

Summary

Violence against women is pervasive in all societies and cultures, and churches are not excluded from the problem. It is vital that churches rise to the challenge and take their place in responding well to survivors, offering safe spaces, and also providing accountability and support to perpetrators of abuse as they take responsibility for their attitudes and actions. It is important that churches do not do this alone but rather actively seek out the advice and professional services available.

May the Church rise up to take action. No longer silent. No longer justifying violence against women with our thoughts or

Crucible January 2015

scriptures. No longer thinking it's not in this church. Rather may the global Church and Christians rise up and make a stand and say this is our business, this is our church. All violence against women is wrong and must stop.

In the words of United Nations Secretary General Ban Ki-moon, 'There is one universal truth, applicable to all countries, cultures and communities: violence against women is never acceptable, never excusable, never tolerable.' (United Nations c)

Mandy Marshall is Co-Founder and Co-Director of Restored.

References

Archbishop: 'Survivors of abuse are never the ones to blame', 1 October 2014, www.archbishopofcanterbury.org/blog.php/21/survivors-of-abuse-are-never-the-ones-to-blame.

Evangelical Alliance: 'How's the Family', Evangelical Alliance report, 2012, www.eauk.org/church/resources/snapshot/hows-the-family.cfm.

Home Office: www.gov.uk/domestic-violence-and-abuse.

Methodist Report: 'Domestic Violence and the Methodist Church – the way forward', Conference Report 2002, www.methodist.org.uk/downloads/conf-domestic-violence-the-way-forward-2002.pdf.

Office of National Statistics a: www.ons.gov.uk/ons/rel/crime-stats/crime-statistics/focus-on-violent-crime-and-sexual-offences-2012-13/rpt-chapter-4-intimate-personal-violence-and-partner-abuse.html.

Office of National Statistics b: 'Focus on: Violent Crime and Sexual Offences 2012/13', ONS, 2014, www.ons.gov.uk/ons/rel/crime-stats/crime-statistics/focus-on-violent-crime/stb-focus-on--violent-crime-and-sexual-offences-2011-12.html#tab-Types-of-violence--domestic-violence--sexual-offences-and-intimate-violence.

Office of National Statistics c: 'Overview of violence crime and sexual offences 2012/2013', ONS, February 2014, http://www.ons.gov.uk/ons/rel/crime-stats/crime-statistics/focus-on-violent-crime-and-sexual-offences-2012-13/rpt-chapter-1-overview-of-violent-crime-and-sexual-offences.html#tab-Summary-of-Homicides-Weapons-and-Intimate-Personal-Violence-IPV-Analysis.

Restored a: Restored is an international Christian Alliance to transform relationships and end violence against women. www.restoredrelationships.org.

Restored b: See 'Ending Domestic Abuse: a pack for churches', Restored, 2011, www.restoredrelationships.org/resources/info/51/.

Restored c: First Man Standing, Restored, http://www.restoredrelationships.org/firstmanstanding/pledge/.

United Nations a: /www.un.org/en/globalissues/briefingpapers/endviol/.

United Nations b: UN Women, 2013, http://www.unwomen.org/en/what-we-do/ending-violence-against-women/facts-and-figures.

United Nations c: UN Declaration on the Elimination of Violence Against Women, 1993; reaffirmed in UN CSW 57 Agreed Conclusions 2013, www.un.org/womenwatch/daw/csw/csw57/CSW57_agreed_conclusions_advance_unedited_version_18_March_2013.pdf.

United Nations d: He For She, UN, 2014 /www.heforshe.org/.

United Nations e: www.un.org/en/globalissues/briefingpapers/endviol/quotes.shtml.

Women's Aid: www.womensaidorg.uk/domestic-violence-articles.asp?.

Masculine Constructions

ALAN PATERSON

Personal prologue

I retain a memory of dad holding mum by her shoulders and hair and shaking her, her head banging against the door behind her. On another occasion he had tried forcibly to eject her from the house. The violence was not habitual, nor was it a systemic attitude towards women in general, but it was my first insight into violence against women, of a man with mental health problems and unreasonable expectations of marriage.

Twice dad spent time in psychiatric institutions and came out temporarily improved, and on another two occasions mum took my sister and me to stay with her mother for a few weeks, when things became intolerable. I was nine when eventually, after a violent incident, mum said she was leaving and would not be back, and dad responded that he was keeping us children. A prolonged process through Edinburgh Sheriff Court meant I was nearly 11 when a legal separation granted my mother custody.

A changing generation

Like others before with hormones on the boil, my generation fumbled and fondled, and sex was a taboo for many. The biology said 'breed' but authority was saying 'no'. Fear of unwanted pregnancy, opprobrium from our critical communities and sexually transmitted infections all added to the pressure to abstain. The newly-available contraceptive pill was beyond our reach, condoms were only available on request from chemists and barbers, and any abortion was illegal, dangerous and backstreet. Members of my generation with a church commitment were taught that pre-marital sex was just wrong. Paul had advised that, 'it is better to marry than to burn' (1 Cor. 7.9), but we were taught the corollary that, until we married, burning was the only option. All of the above led to many of my generation being insecure about sex. Repression, sublimation and frustration skewed courting for both sexes, and boys knew but didn't necessarily understand their own hang-ups let alone those of the girls. The swinging sixties arrived as I turned 15, but sexual liberation was mostly for later arrivals.

Evolving morality

Various influences vied for my attention. A Scout leader introduced me to the Moral Re-Armament movement which taught that life should be lived in accordance with the four moral absolutes of purity, unselfishness, honesty and love. The idealism of the language was highly attractive, but I was leery of its unhealthy interest in the pursuit of celebrity and its American political bias. In 1963 John Robinson published *Honest to God* (Robinson 1963), and, tellingly, my marginal notes of criticism in the early pages disappeared, as I began to glimpse his commitment to a new approach to Christian teaching and ethics. In 1965 I began training for ministry at the Scottish Congregational College, and somewhere during that training we spent a term looking at Joseph Fletcher's *Situation Ethics* (Fletcher 1966). Many, from Augustine of Hippo to John Robinson, had discussed the idea that the only absolute in ethics was the law of love, and that all other principles and ideals derive their validity in so far as they serve the purpose of love. Fletcher argued his case drawing from previous writers. I found his ideas a breath of fresh air, given the codified structure of the ethics my church had offered in my Christian nurture.

Violent men

Violence against women never seemed to hit the headlines during my formative years, but the media had much to say about juvenile delinquency that may not have been unrelated. There was an assumption that males were more inclined towards violence in general. It seemed to be accepted that, from ancient times, men supplied the warriors and armies of societies, tribal or imperial. In the aftermath of an empire and two world wars it seemed males had a dispensation for violence, a prerogative. Scots mercenaries had served in Ireland, Scandinavia and mainland Europe from the Dark Ages until the eighteenth century; clan chiefs had raised regiments for the British Army up till the Napoleonic Wars. Twentieth-century gang culture had old roots.

In 2009 Jóhann Axel Andersen produced the academic paper, 'Casting a Long Shadow — A Study of Masculinity and Hard Men in Twentieth Century Scottish Fiction' (Andersen 2009). He asserts that pride, strength, rigidity and lack of emotion are common characteristics of the Scottish hard man. He seems to suggest that the Scottish Calvinist Reformation, the Scottish Enlightenment, the agrarian and industrial revolutions, urbanization, the wars of empire, the rise of capitalism, the rise of the radical movement/ trade unionism/ socialism followed by the collapse of coal, steel and heavy industries all produced changes and upheavals men had difficulty coping with. The obsolescence of male prowess and the alpha-male performance, the collapse of patriarchal male dominance and the sense of unstable and ever-changing gender roles threatened traditional masculinity. His paper is about fiction, however, and the period examined covers a shift from the Kailyard School's portrayal of a sentimentalized, rural version of Scottish life, towards grotesque realism.

On Being a Man: Four Scottish Men in Conversation (Torrance, Campbell, Seaman and Cornachan 2014) was published in summer 2014. The authors were a writer and broadcaster, the founder of a youth employment and mentoring charity, a public health researcher, and the head of the violence reduction unit, a former policeman. The conversation was fascinating but some Scottish statistics were arresting:

90 per cent of school children with behavioural problems are boys.
80 per cent of school children with learning difficulties are boys.
81 per cent of pupil exclusions are boys.
90 per cent of court appearances are males between 16 and 24.
90 per cent of all violent crime is committed by men.
84 per cent of suicide victims are men aged 16–24.
In the 10 years following the invasion of Afghanistan in 2001, 43 Scottish servicemen lost their lives in conflict. In the same period 5,624 men in Scotland committed suicide.

Andersen's finding that the increasing pace of change has created a continuing crisis for masculinity is further underlined by the *On*

Being a Man, writers who conclude that men making the transition from industrial worker to service-sector job seeker, from doting father to estranged, absent father, from gang member to job seeker/apprentice, from provider to pensioner is equally fraught. Certainly the above statistics indicate that we have not mastered being a man. John Carnochan (Violence Reduction Unit) has asserted what is missing in the personal history of young men from the most deprived areas is a positive male role model, and what is lacking in their envisioned future is work, purpose and meaning. Alcohol and violence were almost always present.

Men's mental baggage

Reasonably early in my ministry a young woman came for advice, because her husband had taken to coming home on a Friday night via the pub with drink taken and a violent tendency. Her mother, who had been twice widowed, told her 'Aye, it's like that.' I was shocked, thinking I knew the family. Male attitudes towards women have a lot of baggage from the past. In the Torah women seem to be regarded as chattels, valued somewhere between the house and the servant in coveting stakes. Property and inheritance law shaped their status, with a need in nomadic times to maintain the breeding stock of the tribe. Rahab, the harlot, and the practice of cult prostitution among Israel's neighbours reflect a utilitarian history of women for men's sexual gratification, while polygamy and concubinage did little to enhance the status of women in men's eyes. From the megalomania of Henry VIII to the cynicism revealed by the present Prince of Wales' attempts to breed royal heirs have not been edifying. Mutuality, love and respect, have been hard to discern. Prostitution and today's massive pornography industry have continued to feed the perception that women are objects of lust.

The sex business

In 2002 the Scottish Parliament considered a proposal to authorize local authorities to set up prostitution tolerance zones. Such an informal zone in Edinburgh had contributed to the safety of street sex workers as well as access to counselling, welfare and health support. Simultaneously in Glasgow the policy of zero tolerance

Crucible January 2015

had driven prostitution underground, and Glasgow prostitutes were being murdered at the rate of almost one per month. Residential redevelopment of the tolerance zone in Edinburgh caused its abandonment and subsequently violent assaults on prostitutes increased tenfold, according to SCOT–PEP (Scottish Prostitutes Education Project, a registered charity dedicated to the promotion of sex workers' rights, health and dignity). In a very deprived area of Glasgow a doctor was clear that the prostitutes seen and treated were often the youngest and most vulnerable: constantly at risk of violence, with mental health, addiction, debt and poverty problems and least family support. By contrast SCOT–PEP believed that sex work can be a positive choice, and that sex workers have the right to work without fear of stigma or oppression. It believes that only rights can stop the wrongs, and that laws to restrict or criminalize sex work have put sex workers at increased risk of violence and abuse.

In 2013 an article appeared in the *Sunday Herald* (McArdle 2013) indicating that about 450 students from Glasgow Caledonian, Edinburgh and St Andrews Universities had signed up for a Sugar Daddies dating website called 'SeekingArrangement', which advertised men offering up to $20,000 (£12,650) a month to women willing to be their 'sugar baby'. The online payment giant PayPal had withdrawn from the scheme calling it too sexual. The site promised to link 'attractive, intelligent, ambitious' young women with 'respectful and generous' older men for a 'mutually beneficial' relationship. It attracted criticism for being a springboard into prostitution by encouraging young women to 'sell themselves'. Brandon Wade, the founder, conceded that the site sits in a 'grey area' somewhere between romantic dating and a business transaction, but rejected the comparison with prostitution claiming it was simply 'being honest' to say men are rated by their earning power, while women are valued by their looks.

On 8 August in 2013, Rebecca Schofield, postgraduate student in Women's Studies at York University posted in the *Huffington Post* 'The Secret World of the Student Sex Worker' (Huffpost a). Much of her material was sourced from the Student Sex Work Project at Swansea University (Swansea). She stated that there had been an increase in the number of students becoming active in the sex industry because of costs and debt, with some students leaving university with a cumulative debt in excess of £50,000. The project identifies sex work as including selling sexual acts for money, such as pole and lap dancing, stripping, web cam and phone chat sex, escort work and massage. The project is to develop and deliver an integrated sexual health service for student sex workers in Wales. Its aim is to promote learning and understanding about student sex worker needs. The article explains: 'It is evident that this kind of work is far from glamorous, and in fact can be incredibly dangerous for students, with the possibilities of STDs, violent punters and, not least, the social repercussions of being found out as a sex worker.' A student sex worker is quoted as saying, 'I know several students who work as escorts. I can make £800 a week, at least. A lot of my student friends meet a guy in a club and sleep with them that night and never see them again – at least I get paid for it.'

New EU rules mean the Office for National Statistics will for the first time have to include illegal activities in its official estimate of the total value of UK gross domestic product (GDP). Based on 2009 prices, the ONS has estimated prostitution will add £5.3 billion to Britain's GDP (Huffpost b).

Strategy

The Scottish Parliament came into being in 1999 and, in lieu of a second chamber, adopted public consultation for assessing proposed policy and legislation. In 2000 the United Reformed Church (URC) inaugurated its National Synod of Scotland (authorized to speak on behalf of the whole URC on domestic Scottish issues), and in turn its Church and Society Committee did the primary work in responding to parliamentary consultations. To date the committee has drafted the Synod's response to 11 consultations, six being about the sexes and a further two about same sex relationships. I was the committee's first convener. In 2003 the Scottish Government issued a draft sexual health strategy, 'Enhancing Sexual Wellbeing in Scotland'. The committee consulted nine professionals ranging from a clinical psychologist to a social worker. Recognizing the problems of increasing numbers of unplanned teenage pregnancies and sexually transmitted infections we welcomed

Crucible January 2015

a strategy for coordinating the work of various agencies and attempting to address both low self-esteem and poor access to information and advice.

The consultation document defined sexual wellbeing in terms of cultural, ethical and spiritual components, but addressing these components seemed to centre on education rather than providing motivation to change. We quoted one consultant: 'motivation to change will only be generated when benefits from behaviour change are perceived to outweigh benefits of the status quo. Longer term implications of "unhealthy" sexual behaviours, like unprotected sex, promiscuity and teenage pregnancy, only carry weight when a young person has sufficient self-esteem to believe in a future where aspirations are achievable.' A doctor had spoken of meeting 'people who do not respect themselves or others, do not act responsibly and do not understand how to protect themselves from the unwanted outcomes of sexual activity'.

Sex as inevitable early in a relationship, sex as an appetite to be fed or even an itch to be scratched, sex equivalent in its casualness to a handshake, sex as a tool for manipulating people, sexual gratification as a right and sexual encounter as conquest all seem to run counter to healthy interpersonal relationships. We emphasized that promotion of healthy interpersonal relationships would be an uphill struggle while these attitudes are regarded as norms. Young people are under great pressure to be sexually active. Sexual imagery pervades much advertising, and the competitive nature of the industry means that the boundaries are always being pushed, salacious stories sell newspapers, the foibles of celebrities sell magazines, gangster rap lyrics tell boys that girls are chattels, and much teenage fashion seems to be about parading sexuality. These unhealthy norms being entrenched in society are the product of major investment, which is ongoing.

Beyond the sexual norms being pushed, there was a dramatic rise in elimination games on television, from 'Castaway', 'The Weakest Link' through 'Pop Idol' to 'Big Brother'. They frequently promote the rejection of other people rather than valuing them, and they imply that life and society are an ongoing competition. Countering not only the attitudes, but also the vested interests that support them, is vital. We urged that ways should be found to affirm that individuals can be healthy and normal when not involved in a sexual relationship, individuals have the freedom to choose when they are ready and consenting to have a sexual relationship, sexual and emotional wellbeing is strongly linked to how people value themselves and each other, good sex usually arises from mutual commitment, and long term, faithful sexual relationships have health benefits. The strategy document mentioned the spiritual dimension of wellbeing but needed to spell it out that this was where values, aspirations and identity could be discussed and perhaps where love could be disentangled from sentimentality or lust.

Concluding our response we said, 'We are aware that churches have in the past been more authoritative than enabling, more prohibiting than affirming, and that churches today are often still perceived to be so. The strategy document has helped us to realize that the Church, along with other faith groups, has a role to perform in lifting its own taboos, in opening up genuine discussion, and in helping young people arrive at a morality they can own. The exercise of responding to the strategy document has helped us to identify our need to be more explicit in affirming the worth of young individuals and their right to make an informed choice about if or when sex is right for them.'

Where next?

Revisiting that response 11 years later, there is little our committee would change, although recognizing failure to pursue our own perceived wisdom reinforces a sense of guilt. The Church has chosen to believe prostitution is an abuse of women, and particularly of those who are emotionally or financially vulnerable; but some wonder whether in a permissive society it can be a liberated woman's career choice. In an age when society has turned its back on sexual taboos and prohibitions, what moral rules or government legislation are appropriate to a twenty-first-century society? Are we as a society any closer to knowing whether prohibition laws would achieve their purpose or simply drive the industry underground? Have we any concept of the vested interests behind the sex industry? Have we any idea whether the sexual liberation of the last 50-odd years has benefited those who might otherwise have become sexually insecure and repressed, or whether it has led to a promiscuous society? Does the word promiscuous indicate more than the disapproval of a previous

Crucible January 2015

generation? Do the sexual entertainment and online pornography industries (as legal, adult activities) merit less condemnation than prostitution, and would we see the grooming of minors and trafficking for sex as the worst threats to be condemned?

All of the above are questions that still hang in the air, some not addressed at all. Behind all of the considerations, however, hangs the question, how do these factors feed the fantasies of those men who continue to see women as objects and sex as a commodity, and whose behaviour reflects those fantasies?

As I was spreading out the odd bits and pieces of my knowledge in this area, looking for some pattern, I began to wonder if attributing things to men and women as gender problems for solving had become an exhausted approach. There are no obvious means whereby men can solve the problems represented in the statistics quoted from *On Being a Man* any more than men have solutions to the problems of adapting to historical, industrial, domestic or sociological changes in their lives. The predominance of women in the sexual entertainment and pornography industries or in the sex trade hardly indicates that women per se can bring about changes in that sphere.

These problems relate to society as a whole, to its politics, economics, values and aspirations, and will not profit from being parked in a locker labelled gender issues. Sandy Campbell, in *On Being a Man* complains: 'There has been a creeping consensus emerging since the sixties that if you are white don't debate what it might be like to be black; if you are male don't profess to know anything about womanhood; and if you are heterosexual don't comment on the gay experience. It is a "Ghetto-ist" position that separates us from common humanity and our daily mixing and relating with that "other", an "other" that we must never have a view on lest we offend, and reassert our white, male, power domination.'

Tantalizingly, towards the end of the book, there is a glimpse of an idea that we should cease to look at gender as 'What we are, in which male and female play off and define one another, consciously or unconsciously' (Torrance, Campbell, Seaman and Cornachan 2014, pp. 107, 109), and instead see it as 'enactment' — as an evolving relationship, if I have understood their point.

Alan Paterson is Secretary of the United Reformed Church Synod of Scotland Church & Society Committee.

References

Andersen, Johann A., 2009, 'Casting a Long Shadow — A study of masculinity and Hard Men in Twentieth Century Scottish Fiction', Sigillum Universitatis Islandiae.

Fletcher, Joseph, 1966, *Situation Ethics: the New Morality*, London: SCM Press.

Huffpost a, 'Secret World of the Student Sex Worker: Huffpost Students, United Kingdom', 8 August 2013.

Huffpost b, The Huffington Post UK/PA | Posted: 30/05/2014 08:07 BST | Updated: 30/05/2014 08:59 BST.

McArdle, Helen, '"Sugar daddy" boss: I support traditional values', *Sunday Herald*, 27 January 2013.

Robinson, J., 1963, *Honest to God*, London: SCM Press .

Swansea: www.thestudentsexworkproject.co.uk/.

Torrance D., Campbell, S., Seaman, P., and Cornachan, J., 2014, *On Being a Man: Four Scottish Men in Conversation*, Edinburgh: Luath Press.

— The Violence of Poverty —

An Exploration of Violence Against Women and Development

CATHRIN DANIEL

Introduction

Poverty, looked at globally, has a woman's face. Despite the huge progress made in global development over the past 50 years, women continue to lag behind men in almost all human development indicators.

It is a scandal that while women constitute half the world's population, the UN tells us that 70 per cent of those living in poverty today are women. Women do 75 per cent of the world's agricultural work, yet they own less than one per cent of the land. They perform nearly two-thirds of the world's work hours, yet receive just one-tenth of its total income. It is a scandal that gender is still one of the most powerful determinants of poverty in the world today. It is also one of the world's great injustices, as no one chooses their own sex, and our gender, being a social construct, is always conferred upon us by others at birth (though many choose to define their gender differently or to change their gender later).

Exacerbating and perpetuating this injustice that holds back not only half the world's population, but all development progress globally, is the scourge of violence against women. Violence against women (VAW) is a global pandemic. It represents the most widespread and persistent violation of human rights worldwide. No woman or girl in the world is immune from its threat. According to a 2013 study from the World Health Organization (WHO), at least one in three women worldwide (35 per cent) will experience physical and/or sexual violence during their lifetime, usually at the hands of someone they know (WHO 2013). This means that more than one billion women worldwide are affected by VAW and its effects are devastating, not only on the individual and her family, but also on all aspects of human development and dignity.

This paper aims to explore the nexus between VAW, poverty and development and what churches can do to respond to this global and local challenge. I suggest that we broaden our understanding of what constitutes VAW to encompass all forms of structural and cultural violence that inhibit women from fulfilling their potential as human beings, created in God's image, and that deprive them of that dignity which God has conferred upon all humankind. And finally I pose the challenge to the church and to all that seek the just and full realization of all human development to be transformative in our approach to tackling all forms of VAW in our families, communities and worldwide and to share with others a vision of gender justice for all humankind that reflects God's love for all his creation.

Violence against women: a global pandemic

Violence against women, in the form of physical and/or sexual violence, affects between 15 and 76 per cent of women in their lifetime. Six out of ten women will experience violence simply because they are women. Most of this violence takes place within intimate relationships, with many women (ranging from 9 to 70 per cent) reporting their husbands or partners as the perpetrator (Unifem a). VAW affects women at all stages of their lives, but tragically, young women and girls are by far the most vulnerable to sexual forms of violence. Worldwide, up to 50 per cent of sexual assaults are committed against girls under 16 (IRCW 2000). The first sexual experience of some 30 per cent of women was forced. Amongst those who were under 15 at the time of their sexual initiation, up to 45 per cent report that the experience was forced (Unifem b).

Whilst all women are vulnerable, poverty, exclusion and war often lead to the erosion of those institutions and infrastructure that can offer women some protection from violence and uphold their human rights, increasing their vulnerability even further.

VAW and development

VAW in all its forms has a direct impact on global poverty. Women and girls represent half the world's human capital in tackling poverty and developing economies, yet physical and sexual violence not only stymies their development and wellbeing, but that of their families, communities and the economic development of whole countries. Poverty and VAW are inextricably linked.

Female mortality

The World Bank estimates that acts of violence against women cause more death and disability worldwide than cancer, malaria, traffic accidents and war combined in the 15-to-44 age group. Every year, more women and girls die globally than men. This disparity is particularly pronounced in low and middle income countries, where females are more likely to die, relative to males, than their counterparts in rich countries. These deaths equate to an estimated 3.9 million additional women and girls under the age of 60 dying each year. Of these

- about two fifths are never born;
- one sixth die in early childhood;
- and over one third die in their reproductive years
  (World Bank 2011).

Overall, the world is missing almost four million women and girls, with deaths in childbirth accounting for about a third of the overall number of missing women (1.35 million out of 3.89). An even bigger share comes from the 1.43 million girls missing at birth, mainly in China and India.

One consequence of this kind of gender discrimination in communities where the practice of sex-selective abortions and female infanticide (the deliberate killing of new-born female children) is common is that families struggle to secure a wife for their sons. Some of the knock-on effects of this further violate women and girls' rights, as it can lead to an increase in the trafficking of women and girls over borders, girl-child abductions and the sale of young girls into domestic slavery and sexual servitude.

Loss of economic productivity and care costs

Amongst the many developmental impacts of VAW are the enormous direct and indirect costs for survivors, employers and the public sector in terms of health, police, legal and related expenditures as well as lost wages and productivity.

According to a study in India, a woman loses an average of at least five paid work days for each incident of intimate partner violence (ICRW 2009), while in Uganda, about nine per cent of violent incidents forced women to lose time from paid work, amounting to approximately 11 days a year (ICRW 2009). In countries that are already struggling with low incomes and developing economies, VAW adds an additional financial burden on the state and on families that they can ill afford. It goes without saying that the victim is not the cause of these costs, but the individual, cultural and structural perpetrators that inflict this harm upon them.

Loss of educational opportunities

Lack of education is one of the biggest barriers to development and one that affects women and girls more than men. Much progress has been made over the last decade to get girls enrolled in primary education, yet 31 million girls worldwide are still not enrolled in primary school. In many of the world's poorest and most unequal countries, the gender disparity at primary and secondary schools remains stubbornly at around two thirds, with this figure increasing with every step up the educational ladder. In sub-Saharan Africa, though there are on average 92 girls per 100 boys enrolled in primary education, this figure drops to 84 at secondary level and to a dismal 61 at tertiary level (Women Deliver).

One of the major causes of school-aged girls dropping out of education is sexual violence. It is staggering that every year 60 million girls are sexually assaulted either at or going to and from school (Moosa et al. 2010). The impact on their education is huge.

School-related violence limits the educational opportunities and achievements of girls. In a study in Ethiopia, 23 per cent of girls reported experiencing sexual assault or rape en route to or from school (Save the Children 2008). In Ecuador, adolescent girls reporting sexual violence in school identified teachers as the perpetrator in 37 per cent of cases (Velásquez and Vargas 2008). In South Africa, 33 per cent of reported rapes of girls were perpetrated by a teacher. Many girls changed schools or left school as a result of hostility after they reported the violence (Department of Health 1999).

Crucible January 2015

The loss of education caused by sexual violence has a hugely detrimental effect on a girl's wellbeing and that of her family. Countless studies have shown that educating girls lifts women and children out of poverty and is a key driver in breaking the cycle of poverty and exclusion:

- When a girl in the developing world receives seven years of education, she marries four years later and has 2.2 fewer children (Levine, Lloyd, Greene and Grown 2009).
- An extra year of primary school education boosts girls' eventual wages by 10–20 per cent. An extra year of secondary school adds 15–25 per cent (Psacharopoulos and Patrinos 2000).

Child marriage

Another key factor driving loss of girls' education and gender inequality is the custom of child marriage. Over 60 million girls worldwide are child brides, married before the age of 18, primarily in South Asia (31.3 million) and sub-Saharan Africa (14.1 million). Violence and abuse characterize married life for many of these girls. Women who marry early are more likely to be beaten or threatened, and more likely to believe that a husband might sometimes be justified in beating his wife (UNICEF 2008). Child marriage represents a gross abuse of human rights and infringes on many of the protections conferred to children by the UN Convention on the Rights of the Child (CRC).

Conflicts can make girls more vulnerable to child marriage. For example, a recent report by UNICEF highlighted the prevalence of child marriage in Jordan, which currently represent 13 per cent of all marriages, a figure that has remained stable for the past decade. The research showed that the prevalence of child marriages among Syrian refugees living in Jordan rose from 18 per cent of total marriages in 2012 to 25 per cent in 2013. Newly released figures now show that this rate has further increased to 32 per cent in the first quarter of 2014. The pre-war figure inside Syria included an average of 13 per cent of marriages involving an under-18-year-old (UNICEF 2008).

The effect of early marriage and childbearing on a young mother and her child's mortality rate are staggering and represent yet another way this abuse of young women and girls impacts their development and that of their family. Due to the physical and psycho-social differences between young and adult females, adolescent girls are twice as likely to die during pregnancy as mothers in their twenties (Bruce 2007) and the child of a mother aged under 18 is 60 per cent more likely to die during its first year than an infant born of a mother aged 19 or over (WHO 2008).

Female genital cutting/mutilation (FGM)

FGM is a form of direct violence and discrimination affecting approximately 100 to 140 million girls and women in the world. In Africa alone, more than three million girls annually are at risk of the practice (WHO 2008b). In Sierra Leone and Ethiopia, two of the countries where the practice is almost universal, the prevalence rate is 90 and 91 per cent respectively (UNICEF 2014). Female genital mutilation/cutting is commonly done to children who are unable to give their consent to the practice. This makes it a brutal violation of their human rights and a breach of the UN's Convention of the Rights of the Child (CRC). It also has a huge toll on women and girls' health and wellbeing, increasing the risks of obstructed labour, childbirth complications, new-born deaths, postpartum bleeding, infections and maternal mortality (WHO 2008b).

Tackling the root causes of VAW

At the root of all these forms of VAW lies a deep and unjust inequality between men and women. This manifests itself globally in many forms of physical and sexual VAW, some of which I have explored above. But there are other forms of less physical violence that stem from this inequality, all of which contribute to the persistent and harmful exclusion and abuse of women.

Johan Galtung, the Norwegian sociologist, mathematician and founder of the Peace Institute in Oslo, promulgated a broader understanding of violence as any way in which a powerful group prevents individuals from achieving their full potential (Galtung 1969). He developed the concepts of structural and cultural violence, the former describing how policies and decisions by one group harms the interests of another, and the latter describing cultural norms and values that justify or legitimize forms of direct (physical and/or sexual violence) and structural violence.

47

Taken together, these concepts of structural and cultural violence can be applied to the issue of VAW globally. These indirect forms of violence perpetrated against women and girls globally lead to an avoidable impairment of their fundamental human needs, and limiting their ability to fulfil their human potential. Any policy, law, belief, or norm that keeps a woman in poverty violates her human rights and dignity. This applies not only to policies and attitudes that actively discriminate against women, such as the denial of women's suffrage, but also applies to those that exclude women by omission and fail to promote their equal development, for example by failing to provide adequate protection for women and girls from physical and/or sexual violence.

Examples of *structural VAW* are seen most clearly in very unequal societies and those in which women's rights are not treated the same as men. However, they can also be more insidious and no country has yet succeeded in eradicating this form of violence completely. Common examples include

- laws or practices that discriminate against women and deny them their rights, for example in the case of succession (inheritance), suffrage, financial independence and land ownership;
- the lack of political representation of women in decision and policy-making bodies;
- the denial of and barriers to education that a majority of women and girls face in lower and middle-income countries;
- women's impaired access to healthcare, and especially where this impacts their reproductive rights;
- women's dominance in low paid, insecure jobs and the pay gap between men and women doing the same work.

Cultural forms of VAW are so pervasive that we rarely recognize them as such. These are global phenomena, touching every sphere of our lives in subtle as well as overt ways. They include

- the sexualization of young women and girls, the commodification of their bodies and the normalization of pornography in popular culture;
- the stigmatization of single and/or childless women and widows, ranging from the derogatory term spinster to accusations of witchcraft and black magic;

Crucible January 2015

- norms of masculinity that champion aggression and the objectification and subjugation of women, from the UK's lads magazines, to the initiation rites and language of gang culture, the open misogyny of many internet trolling and the threat/use of violence to extort sexual favours from women and girls.

Structural and cultural forms of VAW create the conditions that allow for direct, physical and sexual violence to be perpetrated against women. These factors combined, drive the economic, social and political exclusion of women and perpetuate the deep inequalities that exist between men and women globally, marginalizing women from development and trapping them and their families in cycles of poverty that last for generations.

By applying this broader understanding of violence, we see that we cannot tackle direct, physical and sexual VAW, or promote the broader development of women, without also dismantling the drivers of structural and cultural forms of VAW, and that means addressing the issue of inequality between the power held by women and that by men globally.

Imbalances in power relations between men and women drive gender inequality. This has a direct impact on poverty, and how it affects men and women differently.

The fact is that of the 1.4 billion people living in poverty, over 70 per cent of them are women (World Bank 2011). Women are disproportionately affected by poverty for no other reason than their gender. This is an injustice that is caused by unequal power relations between men and women, perpetuated by all forms of structural, cultural and physical/sexual violence against women and girls.

Christianity and gender justice

The Bible says that God made humankind in God's image, male and female, and Christians affirm the equality of men and women in God's sight. This means that every community or culture shaped by Christian theology, with an understanding of the unique and inestimable dignity of each human being, should be one in which women and men live alongside each other in peaceful and just relationship. (Durber 2014)

This articulation of a Christian understanding of what gender justice should look like, reflects Christian Aid's understanding of poverty, as a condition caused by broken and unjust human relationships, be it at an individual, community or national level, and the imbalance of power (and therefore inequality) that comes as a result (Christian Aid 2010).

As our love for our neighbour should reflect God's love for us, addressing the injustices of these unequal relations is core to redeeming our relationship with God. This is why seeking justice for women and men in gender relations is a critical part of our Christian mission. In working with partners both in the UK and globally, Christian Aid is seeking to root out the causes of injustice and poverty, and tackling all forms of VAW is one of the critical and effective means of doing so.

To tackle the issue of VAW, we must address the power imbalance between men and women and create a word that is equitable and just *for both* genders. This requires a transformation: a transformation of cultural, structural and individual norms of behaviour, and a transformation in the relationships between men and women.

To eradicate the scourge of VAW, we must do more than simply seek to help its victims. We must go to its roots and pull them out. In developmental terms, it requires us to go further than simply trying to improve the lot of women within an unequal society. Digging a well, for example, will make the lives of women and girls who collect water daily safer and more productive, but it doesn't change the fact that it is the women who are expected to do unpaid housework, women who are excluded from education and women who are denied access to income and capital that will ultimately transform their lives. If we want to see real equality in our world, to see the eradication of poverty and the advent of peace and justice for all, regardless of their gender, race and age, then we need to address all forms of violence against women and their underlying causes, starting with our own values, attitudes and beliefs.

Transformation and the power of the church

The Church worldwide has a crucial role to play in tackling the root causes of VAW and of restoring just power relations between women and men. The Church wields great influence on the political, social, domestic and spiritual sphere of women and men worldwide. While many Christian teachings and practices have tended to encourage the maintenance of traditional male and female roles, the Church is also a key agent for change in many countries, speaking out against gender injustice and seeking to transform broken relationships between women and men in parishes and communities.

The Church can exert its power to perpetuate gender injustice and VAW, or to empower women and girls and transform the relationships that violate not only their rights and human dignity, but that of men and boys too. By working through church partners worldwide, Christian Aid is transforming gender relations in developing countries and challenging our supporters, faith leaders and politicians here in the UK to reach for a transformative understanding of gender justice.

Christian Aid believes that the Christian faith holds at its heart 'a vision for the righteous and joyful justice among humankind, one in which men and women may flourish and live in peace with one another' (Durber 2014). This is a vision of gender justice, and of God's Kingdom fulfilled in all its glory.

Cathrin Daniel is Head of Christian Aid Wales.

References

Bruce, J., 2007, 'Reaching The Girls Left Behind: Targeting Adolescent Programming for Equity, Social Inclusion, Health, and Poverty Alleviation', prepared for: 'Financing Gender Equality; a Commonwealth Perspective', Commonwealth Women's Affairs Ministers' Meeting, Uganda, June 2007, http://www.popcouncil.org/pdfs/Bruce2007CommonwealthFullText.pdf.

Christian Aid, 2010, 'Theology and International Development', http://www.christianaid.org.uk/images/theology-internationaldevelopment-May2010.pdf.

Department of Health, 1999. *South Africa Demographic and Health Survey*: 99.

Durber, Susan, 2014, *Of the Same Flesh: A Theology of Gender*, http://www.christianaid.org.uk/images/of-the-same-flesh-gender-theology-report.pdf.

Galtung, J., 1969, 'Violence, Peace, and Peace Research', *Journal of Peace Research* 6:3, pp. 167–91.

ICRW, 2000, *Domestic Violence in India: A Summary Report for a Multi-Site Household Survey* 3:18, Washington, D.C.: ICRW.

ICRW, 2009, *Intimate Partner Violence—High Costs to Households and Communities* 11, Washington, D.C.: ICRW.

Levine, R., Lloyd, C., Greene, M., and Grown, C., 2009, 'Girls Count a Global Investment & Action Agenda: A Girls Count Report on Adolescent Girls', Center for Global Development. Girls Count, 2009, http://www.cgdev.org/files/15154_file_GC_2009_Final_web.pdf.

Moosa Z.et al., 2010, 'Destined to Fail? How violence against women is undoing development', Action Aid, https://www.actionaid.org.uk/sites/default/files/doc_lib/destined_to_fail.pdf.

Psacharopoulos, G., Patrinos, H., 2002, 'Returns to Investment in Education: A Further Update', World Bank. Education Economics 12.2: (111–34), http://siteresources.worldbank.org/EDUCATION/.

Save the Children Denmark, Ministry of Education & Ministry of Women's Affairs. 2008. *A study on violence against girls in primary schools and its impacts on girls' education in Ethiopia*: 32, New York: UNGEI.

UNICEF, 2008, *ChildInfo: Statistics by Area: Child Protection*, New York: UNICEF, www.childinfo.org/marriage.html.

UNICEF, 2013, http://data.unicef.org/child-protection/fgmc.

UNICEF, 2014, 'A Study in Early Marriage in Jordan 2014', http://www.unicef.org/mena/UNICEFJordan_EarlyMarriageStudy2014.pdf.

Unifem a: UN's Development Fund for Women (UNIFEM), http://www.unifem.org/gender_issues/violence_against_women/

Unifem b: at http://www.endvawnow.org/en/articles/299-fast-facts-statistics-on-violence-against-women-and-girls-.html.

Velásquez, T. C. and G. M. Vargas, 2008, 'Me too...Sexual Harassment and Abuse in Ecuadorian Schools', CONAMU, Women's Communications Workshop, Quito.

WHO ,2008a, 'Why is giving special attention to adolescents important for achieving Millennium Development Goal 5?', World Health Organization, http://www.who.int/making_pregnancy_safer/events/2008/mdg5/adolescent_preg.pdf.

WHO, 2008b, *Female Genital Mutilation – Fact Sheet No. 241*, Geneva: WHO, www.who.int/mediacentre/factsheets/fs241/en/.

WHO, 2013, 'Global and regional estimates of violence against women: prevalence and health effects of intimate partner violence and non-partner sexual violence', World Health Organization (WHO), London School of Hygiene and Tropical Medicine and South African Medical Research Council.

Women Deliver: http://www.womendeliver.org/knowledge-center/facts-figures/girls-education/.

World Bank, 2011, World Development Report, 2011, http://web.worldbank.org/WBSITE/EXTERNAL/EXTDEC/EX-TRESEARCH/EXTWRS/0,,contentMDK:23252415~pageP-K:478093~piPK:477627~theSitePK:477624,00.html.

Forum

This new Forum part of each future edition of *Crucible* seeks to generate theological reflection on current matters of importance in society and church. Matt Bullimore is its current editor. I hope you will find it useful.

John Atherton, Editor

This second Forum engages with the environment and then the consequences of the Scottish Referendum.

— Climate Change and — the World We Live In

PAUL BALLARD

Introduction

The world has always been subject to variations in weather patterns. There have been major ice ages followed by warm periods and, within recorded history, mini versions of the same. But this time another factor has interfered with and accelerated the natural rhythms. The Panel for Climate Change of the United Nations (September 2013) has clearly demonstrated that global warming is happening and that it is significantly, if not largely, due to human activity. The primary cause is the exponential increase in the release of CO_2 into the atmosphere, the product of our now global and expanding, industrial, carbon fuelled economy. This puts climate change squarely on our shoulders; a responsibility we have to accept.

Here, however, I want to look at a central issue that is seldom openly acknowledged. I want to argue that concern for our planet, meeting the challenge of climate change and our responsibility for it, demands a radical reappraisal of our understanding of ourselves and our relation to the world; what we have learnt from Thomas Kuhn to call a paradigm shift. Many would argue that we are indeed entering into a new cultural era, from modernism to post-modernism (or however it should be named), one of the features of which seems to be a new holism that counters the analytical particularism of the modernist world. If so, then I would want to suggest that environmental concern not only chimes in with it but both contributes to and is undergirded by this emerging perspective and gives substance and direction to the way we face the crisis that confronts us all.

The challenge of ecology

Crucially, ecology, a relatively new discipline, challenges the dominant scientific method that has held sway since the eighteenth century. That method assumed (i) a basically mechanistic view of reality, so scientific knowledge was tested by repeatability; thus, (ii) it undertook a search for the fundamental laws and processes that informed this reality; and (iii) was based on an analytical approach that broke reality down into its essential building blocks, assuming that reality was merely the sum of its parts. This approach, dominated by mathematics, physics and chemistry, has opened up our understanding of the universe. But ecology, in contrast, seeks to see the organism holistically as part of a living system. Thus a pond becomes more than a location for particular flora and fauna but is seen as an eco-system of mutual dependencies that can easily be disturbed and is open to change. Such a shift, however, was not so radical for the biological sciences where the theory of evolution had already posited the importance of history and diversification.

Thus ecology, and its subsequent development into environmental sciences, has tended to be understood as part of the biological sciences. That pond, the local eco-system, is itself set in a wider context not least of human activities such as farming. Once the human dimension is brought into play, we are in the realm of personal and social actions and what governs human activity. It is now widely accepted, therefore, that it is impossible for ecological discourse to avoid issues of economics and social policy. It cannot stop there, however, because personal and social choices are themselves governed by assumptions about what human nature is, how we are related to the natural order, and our understanding as to how the universe ticks, which is the substance of metaphysics. Thus the ecological chain stretches from the decline of the natter-jack toad to the CERN in Switzerland, from the hungry in Africa to the ways our urban living operates.

Joining up the dots

There is, therefore, a greater awareness that the health of the planet and human welfare interlock. But progress is painfully slow, running as it does against long held assumptions, political rivalry, clashes of interest and the jostling for economic advantage. If, however, politics is the art of the possible then it may be that the only way forward is by tackling issues in bite-sized portions, taking a step at a time. The danger here, however, is of disconnected, even conflicting, initiatives leading to fragmentation and a loss of cohesion and direction. A coherent and overarching vision that governs and gives coherence to the piecemeal actions is demanded. It is necessary to join up the dots. Without that the picture is simply a mess or, at best, vague.

Perhaps that chasm of discontinuity is at its widest between the needs of the environment and the workings of the economy. The collapse of the world economy in 2008 could have been, as some hoped, an opportunity, to reform radically the runaway financial system that holds us all in thrall. However, there seems to have been little, though some, change in the governance and practices in the financial sector. Above all there is no vision as to how the economy can work differently. The search for recovery has simply been recast in terms of growth. We are also seeing the re-establishment of practices that created the problem in the first place, such as unsecured credit. Such a model of the economy is essentially expansionist and, if left unbridled, totally destructive of the environment. But, it is argued, this is the only game on the block. The green shoots of alternatives are as yet tentative and incoherent. If we are to shift from classic capitalist economies, and socialist economies were no better, then there needs to be a radical change in our understanding as to how the economy should work.

In the first instance it is necessary to make axiomatic the mutuality between the environment and human activity. The earth is widely regarded as a free good, a source from which to draw for our consumption. The waste we produce is a problem on land, in the oceans and in the air, and even in space. But we are guardians and trustees. The natural world is not there simply for our own benefit but needs to be cared for as, at least, a partner in our existence. We are part of nature and dependent on its diversity and health.

Second, there has, therefore, to be a curbing of demand. Much can be done by efficiency and diversification but in the end it is necessary to limit consumption, material and energy demands to sustainable proportions. We need to understand the meaning of enough.

Third, the economic enterprise has to acknowledge its holistic responsibilities. At present, for public companies, the only obligation is to the shareholder, that is, profit, often for short-term gain rather than for long-term sustainability. There is some recognition of the employee and the customer but until recently very little obligation to the wider community or the environment. And it is precisely these requirements that are so easily eroded in times of economic stringency. Pressure has to be asserted to ensure that all the costs are properly and adequately understood and met.

Fourth, the financial market has to be more closely integrated into and to serve the real economy. This implies much closer regulation and control of tax regimes.

Fifth, there is the matter of population growth that puts ever increasing pressure on resources, especially as personal and national expectations are still rising. It is impossible to avoid the controversial issues of population control, with all the cultural, religious and political hazards involved.

Sixth, it is necessary to look afresh at the place and function of technology. It is literally possible to move mountains and to employ nanotechnology and genetic engineering; to probe the vastness of space and plumb the depths of the sea. Knowledge is power but we need to reject the assumption, to parody Kant, that because we can therefore we ought. Our power over nature and into space is a gift and responsibility. Ethical wisdom for playing about with the natural processes, delicate and complex as it is, is needed desperately.

Seventh, and by no means least, there is interwoven in all this a question of justice. It is the poor who tend to have to carry the greater burden, both in climate change and the exploitation of resources. Sustainability has to be an essential element in the search for equitable access to food shelter, security and services.

Faith in the environment

The description of the holistic nature of ecology drives us to look beyond the natural and the economic to the metaphysical, to those beliefs and principles that inform our behaviour. People and communities live according to fundamental beliefs, what Clifford Geertz calls the deep meaning that undergirds their practices. These make up what George Lackoff terms the frame that gives coherence to the manifold and apparently random events of life. We are in this regard, as in so much else, at a time of transition in a maelstrom of competing faiths and philosophies. Yet this task is vital if there is to be any hope of remoulding the future of the planet.

I would like to suggest that there are four main responses to the threats of climate change. These can be looked at as a discrete series, though clearly there is overlap, working from the immediate to the more inclusive and profound.

The first and obvious and dominant reaction is gradualism. It is assumed that the system can be tamed and brought under control;

that it should be possible to hold the market in creative tension with the demands of sustainability. Such measures may seem radical but are really palliative, designed to advance the cause of sustainability through, for example, transport policies, alternative sources of power, technological innovation, recycling and various forms of localism. But such an approach does not really tackle the radical change needed. The hope here is life will continue more or less as normal at minimal cost. Politically it is easier to nibble away at the edges, than to pose the sharp and controversial questions.

Second, human nature is seen as essentially communal and collaborative, seeking, to borrow a Catholic concept, the common good, with special regard for the weak and disadvantaged. This was the vision that inspired the welfare state. This perspective can be enlarged to include the natural environment so that human activity has to be proportionate and responsible. It recognizes the need for sustainable practices, the importance of biodiversity and the conservation of resources. This is probably where most conservation societies (such as the RSPB or WWF) and much voluntary work are found. Such an approach, however, even if there is much overlap with the first in practical activity, is in tension with it, because there is a desire is to enter into a radically new phase of cultural practice.

Third, at another level, there has been a burgeoning of alternative life styles: from an interest in spirituality from Hindu, Buddhist and Celtic spiritualities, to a rediscovery of aboriginal cultures; from a revival of paganism to a simple pantheistic mysticism. This often manifests itself in terms of counter-cultural living, which means it can thus be seen as marginal to, or even parasitic on, mainstream society. Nevertheless, humanity is understood as being embedded in nature and can, at its best, provide a powerful witness to an alternative style for society.

Fourth, the theistic, so called Abrahamic religions have a doctrine of creation. They point to an understanding of humanity as essentially part of the created order, made out of the stuff of the earth. At the same time humanity also stands, before God, in a special relation to the earth in which it is set. This makes us responsible to God in and for the world. The notion of dominion in Genesis (1.28) acknowledges humankind's power over the earth but, properly understood, it is given that the earth may flourish and prosper. The world is seen as a garden that has to be tended and which yields food and shelter and all else that is needful for human wellbeing, yet is a home where the other creatures too have their proper place. Thus there is both a relation to the earth and a creativity in its use.

In the Judaeo-Christian tradition there are two other factors. First, the relationship has broken down. Sin destroys the balance. The use of God's gifts has been to dominate and control. So in this narrative the powers of selfishness and greed are really and readily acknowledged, though not as an essential part of human nature, which must be overcome, though not without a struggle. Second, at the same time there is redemption and hope; the possibility that it is all worth striving for. We are made for peace, *shalom*, which is a rich vision of harmony between people and with nature in the presence of God. This is the true grain of the universe. Here, in this story, there is a wisdom, a point of reference, that affirms and makes it is possible to live in the inevitable tension between threat and hope, to be able to work creatively while struggling with the real issues of power and conflict.

We are set in a time of crucial decision. If we continue as we are then the future looms darkly. Perhaps there is time to change but time is short.

Paul Ballard is Professor Emeritus at Cardiff University.

— Renewing the Union — after the Scottish Referendum

'Mixed Government' and the Crucial Role of the Established Church

Adrian Pabst

The Scottish Referendum has highlighted in dramatic ways the limits of liberal, representative democracy and the case for a federal union with devolved powers to localities and regions under the aegis of the monarchy and the Church.

On the one hand, the two-year campaign confirmed not only the deep seated popular distrust of the Westminster elites but also the desire for genuine alternatives to the established order and demands by a reenergized electorate for substance rather than sound bites. But on the other hand, the official referendum debate quickly turned into a dispiriting contest between the populism of the SNP and the technocracy of the Better Together team, with the former portraying an independent Scotland as a progressive heaven on earth, while the latter issued a serious of warnings and thinly veiled threats including no common currency, no fiscal solidarity, and no automatic membership in the European Union ... The Yes campaign certainly defied initial expectations and had the No camp on the ropes, but in the end a silent majority in favour of the Union made its voice heard.

Now the UK now faces constitutional chaos, as the pledge by the Tory, Labour and Lib-Dem leaders to devolve more powers to the Scottish Parliament has intensified long standing resentment about the under presentation of England within the Union. In response, David Cameron has promised English votes for English laws, whereas Ed Miliband is calling for a constitutional convention to draw up a new settlement.

The problem with Mr Cameron's proposal is that it creates two classes of MPs, those from English constituencies voting on all matters and those from Scottish voting only on UK wide matters, and potentially leads to a bifurcated government. If, say, the Labour Party won a narrow victory in a General Election with the help of its Scottish MPs, then it would have a UK majority for non-devolved matters, such as overall taxation or foreign affairs, but lack the ability to legislate on English matters. 'But a bifurcated government is a logical absurdity. A government must be collectively responsible to parliament for all the policies that come before it, not just a selection of them', as the constitutional expert Vernon Bogdanor has rightly warned (Bogdanor 2014).

Those who object that this puts England at a disadvantage forget that no Union can survive without a single, overarching government prepared to act in concert and with some sense of collegiate solidarity. With two classes of MPs and a bifurcated government, MPs from outside England would not realistically be able to serve as Prime Minister or Chancellor, when in the past as many as eleven British PMs have come from Scotland. All these implications could potentially tear the union asunder and reopen the question of Scottish independence that the referendum was supposed to have settled for at least a generation. So English votes for English laws is a recipe for US-style gridlocked government, the dissolution of the Union and a one party English state. In short, it is anti-unionist and separatist, reinforcing the impression that the Conservative Party leadership is retreating to a Little England stance and revelling in splendid isolation, especially if it takes the UK out of the EU in 2017, which would also galvanize those clamouring for another plebiscite on Scotland.

Miliband's idea of a constitutional convention has the merit of avoiding a quick fix in favour of a longer term reflection and possibly allowing popular involvement in the process. However, such a convention resembles much more the revolutionary regimes of the United States or France than the mixed government model that has served Britain for centuries. Presumably the proposals drawn up by a convention would be put to a vote by the people, but the 2005 EU constitutional treaty dreamt up by politicians and technocrats reveals the dangers of going down this route. Of course, plebiscites have their role and place in a vibrant democracy, but the UK has avoided political extremism precisely by sticking to parliamentary sovereignty, bringing together the crown, the Church and the citizenry in parliament.

More fundamentally, critics of the unwritten British constitution claim that only a fully-fledged federal system with a strict separation of powers would be able to resolve these issues, but such a formal federalism does not sit easily with Britain's traditions of mixed government and the informal, organic ties between the four nations of England, Scotland, Wales and Northern Ireland. Nor has formal federalism linked to a written constitution prevented the concentration of wealth and power at the central level in federal systems such as that of the United States. Crucially, liberal appeals to abstract principles such as equality or fairness fail because they ignore the traditions, institutions, and relationships that can give substantive meaning to formal rules and procedures.

For Britain, this means that democracy and the Union can only be revived in line with the traditions and institutions of mixed government, for example as the interplay of the one, the few, and the many – or, in short, the monarchy, the aristocracy and the people. The monarchic one and the aristocratic few includes much more than a seemingly arbitrary, disproportionate role for those who benefit from hereditary privilege. Even today, monarchy and aristocracy encompass a vast array of corporate bodies under royal and lordly aegis whose constitutional autonomy, relatively non-partisan continuity, and openness to more informal modes of participation balance and qualify the formally sovereign power of the executive and the populace. This, coupled with intermediary institutions, has generated a polity of free association that contrasts radically with the oscillation between the controlling centre and the controlled individuals so beloved of unadulterated liberalism. Key to Britain's mixed government is the Established Church, which is itself a polity and which qualifies the power and authority of the state as something less than absolute and final.

Anglican establishment sustains the idea that the Church is itself a polity and indeed the heart of the English polity, since sacramental coronation alone ultimately conveys legitimacy upon a regime and a constitution that remains creatively unwritten. Thus the English and Scottish states are turned inside out. Their own most inner identity and authority is after all not their own but rather something remotely as well as intimately other to which they are answerable. Secular alternatives can propose a *tempering* of sovereignty from outside, but only a religious conception can propose a tempering at its very core which amounts to a paradoxical (un)foundation. Thereby the authority of the English and Scottish polities, and so effectively the British state, is defined from the outset as self-qualified. The state is ultimately provisional, if I may venture a paradox. It is a polity only because it stands within, and defers to, a polity inclusive of the nation but wider than the nation, a polity of not just global but also cosmic and even eternal extent.

As part of an eternal polity, the Church of England, which in its catholic aspect is in excess of the national polity, is able to uphold *both* religious freedom *and* the secularity of politics. For by grounding the polity in an initial distance from itself, the Church defends the importance of an assent of conscience beyond legality or coercive constraint not as something that should be tolerated but as something that should be valued, the most primary point of political reference. Anglicanism represents one particular religious option assented to by a national majority until the recent past and perhaps less so in future, but the perceived basis of the collective assent in individual conscience logically requires respect for all consciences, including dissenting ones – as has come to be accepted in the course of time and was advocated by some Anglicans from the early modern outset. By contrast, a purely secular grounding of freedom of conscience either dilutes faith, as in the vague religiosity of America's civil religion, or else it relegates faith to the private sphere as in France's version of *laïcité*.

In this manner, the established Church of England does not so much undermine secular politics as help to defend the principle of secularity against either aggressive secularism or religious fundamentalism. Together with the anointed monarchy it qualifies the authority of the State as less than final and absolute, yet also upholds its regional secular legitimacy including the space for religious diversity and toleration. Nor is this enabling of general religious freedom merely negative in character because the higher space of church polity is also one that other denominations can participate in. Indeed, faiths can come to occupy in a quasi-established fashion, thereby coming to exercise a positive social and political influence in the name of their own beliefs. This has already become true for Catholic and Jewish spokespersons and is becoming truer also for Islamic ones.

Equally, the grounding of the British Union within a higher polity ensures that the state will be regarded as merely man made, provisional

65

and always revisable. Just because the realm of England is somehow constitutionally ecclesial in character, its more secular apparatus is *radically* secularized and cannot be sacralized in the manner that has accrued to the French and American constitutions. The political role of the Established Church is therefore neither to sanctify the state nor to supplant the government as elected and representative, but rather to inform public institutions in the direction of both individual virtue and public honour, without which democracy cannot function or thrive.

Fundamentally, the Church as the inserted national presence of a more universal community does not aim to be a rival government. This provides a basis not just for it to bear prophetic witness, which on its own can become tiresomely priggish, moralistic and irrelevant, but also to begin to craft and insist in crafting superior human practices, more ambitious for the convivial beyond mere co-existence than is generally possible for the political arm.

Establishment therefore allows the interplay of the state's coercive powers and the Church's persuasive powers in ways that are both mutually limiting and mutually reinforcing. Equally, it sustains some balance between critical distance and a fruitful insemination. For its established status gives the Church of England a constitutional role in the wider governance of societies and people, both their bodies and their souls, in terms of marriage, death, the care of families, welfare and educational provision.[1] It does so in a manner that avoids reducing people to bare individuals who are abstracted from the relational bonds of nature, family and tradition. It is for all these reasons that the established church cannot simply be dismissed as an expression of some private interest or a communal conspiracy against the nation. On the contrary, it helps nurture the bonds of trust and cooperation that hold society together, besides providing the secular with its necessarily constitutive self-critical distance.

But not only does establishment sustain the secular aspect of the state, it also serves, or should serve, to remind that the only justification for democracy is ultimately theological. For Christian theology, because the people is potentially the *ecclesia*, and since nature always anticipates grace, truth lies finally dispersed amongst all the people, although they this needs to be informed by virtuous guidance, which may be narrowly or widely dispersed. That is because, for the legacy of Christian theology, the Holy Spirit speaks most

Crucible January 2015

infallibly through the voice of all. This may seem like a matter just for Christians, yet it is just this doctrine which seems to square the circle from an arising *aporia* concerning democracy and truth.

Historically, with the new prominence given to the democratic virtues of faith, hope and charity, which all can exercise, unlike Homeric military prowess, or Aristotelian magnanimity of the noble and wealthy, *vox populi* had now become more emphatically *vox Dei*. One can here argue that much modern representative democracy, for example, in Scandinavia, Switzerland, the low countries, Italian and German cities, besides the British Isles, is an evolution from this medieval constitutionalism, a process to which the revolutionary legacies of France and the United States are more irrelevant, or are themselves more indebted, than we often imagine. As Krzysztof Kieślowski's film *Blue* suggests, liberty, equality and fraternity are both unthinkable without, and less crucial than, the theological virtues of faith, hope and charity. For in order to pursue justice, we must believe that the discovery and implementation of justice is objectively possible, just as we must believe in the reality of the human spirit and hope that all the capacities of each and every human spirit will eventually be fulfilled. If this faith is justified, then fraternity will prove more than a vain sentimental gesture through the realization of charity in human reconciliation.

Finally, the Church and crown bind the ecclesial polity to the public realm, whether to the crown-in-parliament at the top or via the parochial system to local government at the bottom. Rather than a formal separation of powers so beloved of secular liberals, which leads either to paralysis or the dominance of the executive, a renewed vision of mixed government can transform the union in line with Britain's best traditions, starting with the devolution of powers to localities and regions across England and the rest of the UK. Since late modern liberal representative democracy seems increasingly incapable of taking decisions in the long term national interest of Britain, or indeed other countries, it falls to other institutions to take the lead, including the monarchy, the House of Lords and the Church of England along with other faith communities and civic movements such as Citizens UK.

Adrian Pabst is Senior Lecturer in Politics at the University of Kent.

Crucible January 2015

Reference

Bogdanor, V., 'Why English votes for English laws is a kneejerk absurdity', *Guardian* 25 September 2014, http://www.theguardian.com/commentisfree/2014/sep/24/english-votes-english-laws-absurdity-separatist.

Note

1. As a polity in its own right, the Church of England's social, charitable, educational and cultural involvement is not simply a religious imperative. It is also a unique contribution to society and a source for great good to the whole nation, to people of all faiths and none. For the Church is the only institution that provides assistance universally and unconditionally. Ecclesial help is not a cover for bible-bashing proselytism but instead embodies Christian gift-exchange, gifts born of both faith and works, offered in love, and given in the hope that they might encourage a giving society. See John Milbank and Adrian Pabst, 'The Anglican Polity and the Politics of the Common Good', *Crucible: the Christian Journal of Social Ethics*, January–March 2014, pp. 7–15.

Book Reviews

Stories from the Street: A Theology of Homelessness

David Nixon
Ashgate, 2013, pp. 208, pbk, £19.99

David Nixon's book is an important, creative, and indeed inspiring piece of practical theology and empirical action research. Leaving the particular content aside for a moment, the approach he takes, and the methodology he employs, offers important and useful insights for those engaged in reflective practice in other ministerial contexts. Whilst the author falls into a few of the common epistemological and ethical ditches hidden within the terrain of theological action research, the book is clearly written, offering an invitation, maybe even an imperative, to those engaged in ministry to listen more attentively to the voices on the margins.

Part One of his book offers the reader theological insights into the nature and importance of story. For Nixon, the telling of one's own story is a valid and useful tool for understanding and gaining insight into the self, and discovering one's place in the world. Much of what is said here has been said elsewhere before, but is important, nonetheless, in creating the lens through which the light which emanates from the particular life stories of his interviewees is reflected and refracted. Here also, Nixon details his methodological approach. Qualitative research methods in the form of semi-structured interviews are used to extract data from the living human documents which are his participants. Such established approaches are normative and ubiquitous, yet the theologian has a particular obligation to at least consider something of the ethical implications of the outsider parachuting in to conduct research on a group for the purposes of pursuing doctoral studies or writing a book. I found it fascinating that it was only in a chance meeting with one of the homeless people featured in the book, but not interviewed formally, Simon, that Nixon hears his own story emerging (pp. 7, 181). Here, for the first time Nixon begins to consider and engage auto-ethnographically with his own positionality, his *Vorteutl*, to borrow from Gadamer, or in other word his own prejudices and preferences as a subjective self: a curate, an outsider, a person who has a home, the one who asks the questions, the one in a position of power.

Crucible January 2015

Part Two of the book is where the precious stones are mined out of the hard rock. This is where Nixon introduces us to his homeless participants, where we hear their voices, and where the author engages with the themes that emerge from the interviews. The theme of biography, or the telling of one's own life story, with a particular emphasis on the point of crisis emerges first. I was intrigued that the author didn't engage with a theology of testimony here. Then themes of emotion and spirituality are unpacked. The final area of consideration is of themes that emerge from reading the Bible contextually with homeless people. This was a wonderful chapter, and its implications for reflective practitioners working in other contexts is significant. But Nixon doesn't engage with the hows or whys which led him to choose those particular passages of Scripture. Also, he is the one who chooses. I wonder what themes would have emerged if the homeless participants had chosen Scriptures to discuss? More significantly, Nixon hasn't engaged with the epistemological problems of thematic analysis. The language of themes emerging is epistemologically problematic, as it presupposes that meaning resides within a text, meaning is hidden away inside the transcript, and the role of the researcher is to extract it or mine it out from the data. It is a passive account of the process of analysis, and it denies the active role the researcher always plays in identifying those patterns and themes. Here Nixon's role as interviewer in creating meaning is down played, and consideration is not given to how he as researcher is vying for hermeneutical priority in the creation of meaning. However, I really liked how Nixon included a short life story of the interviewees. This seems to be something of an afterthought, stumbled upon almost by accident (p. 43), but actually is an enormous strength of the book, for now we can identify with the interviewees not as objects of ministry, or projects with problems, but we connect with them in their totality; real people situated in real life contexts. I would have loved Nixon to have included an addendum in which the 12 homeless people he interviewed had a chance to respond to his interpretation of their interviews, offering the work back to the participants, and thus completing the action research cycle back into praxis.

In this unexpectedly moving book, Nixon calls each and every reader to engage in attentive listening to those voices found on the margins, the often suppressed, quieted, and chaotic voices, for it is there the voice of a homeless God can be heard.

James Harding, St Mellitus College, London

Crucible January 2015

Religion, Society and God: Public Theology in Action

Richard Noake and Nicholas Buxton (eds)
SCM Press, 2013, pp. 160, pbk, £25.00

This is an edited volume based on three years' worth of St Wilfrid public lectures from 2009 to 2011 based at Ripon Cathedral. There is inevitably an eclectic approach taken by the different contributors to the theme of religion and contemporary society, from a variety of faith and post-religious traditions, which is possibly why the collection is badged as public theology, that these are public lectures addressing public issues of the day from a perspective that includes a religious component.

The volume opens with three heavyweight contributions from the Abrahamic traditions, discussing the challenges presented to theology by the modern age. Thus Richard Harries sees serious atheism, for example the existential atheism of Samuel Beckett and the T. S. Eliot of *The Wasteland* rather than the fundamentalist atheism of a Richard Dawkins, as essential to the deep and silent faith that will inspire people back to religion. Dan Cohn-Sherbok suggests that in order to relieve the paradox of how an omnipotent and benevolent God allowed his own people to suffer such terrible degradation in the Holocaust, we need to accept that God lies beyond human comprehension. His chapter finishes with the silence of Job in the face of the unfathomable mystery that is Divine Reality as Divine Reality, rather than as humans conceive it out of their own thought and experience. Mona Siddiqui meanwhile eloquently draws out how Islam conceives of God's love and the basis of the human-divine relationship. She concludes; 'The Qur'anic verses on love are not concerned with sacrificial or redemptive love ... In Islam our earthly destiny is not a punishment, but must be regarded as the beginning of our moral awakening ... what God really wants is for humankind never to lose hope in him' (p. 41).

Other contributors include Daphne Hampson, who details the pernicious impacts of entrenched patriarchy within religious hierarchies on the lives of women and which, in her opinion, are deeply offensive and contradictory in a modernizing world. However, her appeal to spirituality to replace religion is under-developed, and she seems innately wedded to a view of modernism seemingly untouched by the critiques of post-modernism and post-secularism, for example, that the modern world of the twenty-first century is one where 84 per cent of the world's population are estimated to affiliate to a religious

Crucible January 2015

identity. David Jaspers argues that the role of both art and religion is to ground and inspire society by pointing to a deeper grammar and mystery in the face of much of the contemporary shallowness and materialism of contemporary culture. However, his citing of the work of the Chinese artist Ding Fang as a modern exemplar of this capacity is never explained or developed.

More pithy and engaged is Roger Trigg's crunchy analysis of the current relationships between religion, democracy and equality legislation. His critique is that freedom to practice religion in the public sphere plays second fiddle to other forms of human rights judgements on the grounds that it is considered a matter of choice rather than an objective characteristic. He is also criticizes the legal system for defining what religious identity is too narrowly by restricting the notion of freedom of religion to that of freedom of worship. For Trigg this is the start of a slippery slope whereby freedom *of* religion becomes freedom *from* religion in society at large: 'Religious belief becomes a subjective preference which cannot be justified in the public square … the idea that it can contribute positively to discussions about the common good is jettisoned.' (p. 98)

In conclusion, this is an entertaining and thought-provoking collection of essays exploring the often contested and misunderstood relationship between religion, secularity, democracy and the modern state. To call this volume a contribution to public theology is probably misleading due to its eclectic and unsystematic approach. Its strength actually lies in the fact that this is an accessible collection of essays aimed at a wider audience who are perhaps confused and sceptical at the same time, that lies outside the Church and theology. To that end I think this volume has been mispackaged, which is a shame.

Chris Baker, William Temple Foundation and University of Chester

Reinventing Liberal Christianity

Theo Hobson
Eerdmans, 2014, pp. vii + 332, hbk, £19.99

As someone who has been both dismissed and extolled as a *liberal,* I found this book engaging, puzzling and frustrating by turns. Maybe the problem is one of semantics. Hobson is fond of stipulative definitions. *Liberal Protestantism* has classically been applied as a term to late nineteenth and early twentieth century German and American theologians in the period from Schleiermacher to Schweitzer. In contrast, Hobson uses the term to cover a far wider range of thinkers. In addition, rather as cardiologists now speak of good and bad cholesterol, so Hobson talks of good and bad Liberal Protestantism. Even his definition of Liberal Christianity is stipulative, seeking to link Christian theology with the modern Liberal state.

The book's range is very broad, extending back to Christianity's emergence from Judaism, followed by an acute analysis of the Reformation, the Enlightenment and then the modern period. Hobson clearly began with a thesis which he would use history to substantiate. The essence of this thesis is that Christianity rejected Judaism's theocratic union of religion and politics and instead rooted belief in being in Christ. In this Hobson stands very much in the mainstream of contemporary Pauline studies. The shift which came with Constantine was thus a reversal of what the message of Jesus was about. Hobson traces similar aberrations back beyond the Reformation including a critique of the growth in the Church's power by Joachim of Fiore and others.

There follows an interesting and swashbuckling survey of reformation thinkers and then a similar analysis of post-Enlightenment philosophers and theologians. *Bad* liberal protestantism, for Hobson, undervalues the sacraments, and Enlightenment rationalism is seen as a particular demon lending subsequently to various forms of deism. Hobson's reading and scholarship is impressive, and he is confident in his analyses of English, American and mainland European thinkers in these different periods. His liberalism is not that of reductionism and non-realism. An analysis as broad as this is bound to be thinner in some periods, and his treatment of the tractarians and the influence of John Henry Newman on modern theology is less reliable. Similarly, too easily, he places Reinhold Niebuhr on the edge of the Barthian school.

However, the book is a welcome tilt at the neo-conservative reaction of the past generation of theologians and its real concern for Christianity to engage critically with the modern state is equally encouraging.

The conclusion is disappointingly brief, only seven pages, and so there is a sense in which this book is something of a ground clearing exercise, a prolegomenon to a new liberal Christianity/liberal theology. Following this analysis, what might a reinvented liberal

Crucible January 2015

Christianity look like? Surprisingly, Hobson engages only tangentially with orthodoxy and Roman Catholicism. It is particularly surprising that he omits any reference to the catholic modernists, working at the turn of the nineteenth and twentieth centuries. The hints which Hobson gives of his intended new world fall far closer to a reformed catholicism, where the sacraments remain of the essence of the church and help order its critique of wider society. A critical review of Hobson's enterprise here is not meant to be negative of the exercise itself. Instead the issue might be: set out the new vision and offer an interpretation of its place within the wider panorama of western catholic Christianity of which most liberal protestants, good and even *bad*, would have seen themselves as part.

Stephen Platten, Cornhill, London

Mammon's Kingdom: An Essay on Britain, Now

David Marquand
Allen Lane, 2014, pp. 276, hbk, £20.00

Political philosophy and commentary from David Marquand is always challenging, engaging and accurate in its perceptions. His latest book is no exception and is already eliciting both positive and negative critiques from the right and left of the political spectrum. At the heart of this critique of the current state of British society is his concern about the shift from what he describes at one point as tamed capitalism to the market dominated, unregulated capitalism of the past 30 years.

Marquand begins with an analysis which is classical to his general approach. He describes key groups, or élites, over the past century and a half which led to the emergence and success of the post Second World War economic and political consensus. This consensus included the predominant Keynesian economic pattern, a mixed economy of public and private ownership of industry, commerce and service industries, and finally a commitment of all major parties to the welfare state. These élites include what he calls the clerisy of highly educated intellectuals; the second group was a professional public service élite, and then finally he includes a working class élite including Aneurin Bevan, Ernest Bevin, Walter Citrine and others. These helped create the public realm which is a realm of service, equity, professional and public duty. This realm he contrasts with the market realm of buying and selling and the private realm of love, family and friendship.

In the early chapters of this book, Marquand demonstrates how the public realm has been eroded by the shift to faith in a market-oriented state, founded loosely on Chicagoean economic theory which believes it traces itself to the work of Friedrich Hayek. It is a shift that has led to an unprecedented dominance of hedonism and greed, an uncritical individualism and a collective amnesia; a historical perspective has been largely abandoned. The two key figures in this are Margaret Thatcher and Tony Blair, although all governments since the 1980s have effectively embraced similar principles. Ironically, the very moral principles which Blair and Thatcher espoused and sought after have been eroded by their own policies.

Marquand's three political-philosophical heroes are Edmund Burke, John Stuart Mill and R. H. Tawney. These three span the political spectrum. Marquand argues that our current marketized state is divorced from any clear societal moral purpose. Although a self-confessed unbeliever, he is content to argue that it is religion that can help underpin a return to some sense of moral purpose. He is fascinated and encouraged particularly by the way in which Christianity has constantly adapted itself over the past 2,000 years, and he looks to both Roman Catholic and Anglican social ethical teaching. Marquand does not seek a nostalgic, sentimental return to an earlier culture. Instead he calls for a historical perspective and a quarrying of the tradition to help build a renewed critical capitalism rooted in a moral vision. His final sentence captures his challenge succinctly: 'We can't go on as we are.'

Stephen Platten, Cornhill, London

Strange Glory: A Life of Dietrich Bonhoeffer

Charles Marsh
SPCK, 2014, pp. 528, pbk, £16.99

2015 marks the seventieth anniversary of the death of Dietrich Bonhoeffer, one of the twentieth century's most widely read and yet most enigmatic theologians. Few other theologians have had not one but three major biographies dedicated to them, in addition to a substantial body of larger and smaller studies of his work by a wide range of scholars from a wide range of contexts. Thus it would not seem odd to ask what another biographical study of what is no doubt a fascinating albeit short life could add to what cynics call the Bonhoeffer industry if one could read the magisterial works of Bethge and Schlingensiepen.

Yet, I found myself pleasantly surprised and drawn into reading about what I thought to be familiar and well-trodden territory. Marsh is no doubt the greatest living scholar engaging with Bonhoeffer's work. He relies on and acknowledges Bethge and Schlingensiepen, but bases his own work on extensive research of the extant primary and secondary sources. Marsh is sympathetic to his subject but by no means a hagiographer. He writes with profound understanding of the world that shaped Bonhoeffer.

The result is indeed *A Life of Dietrich Bonhoeffer*, an account of the intellectual and emotional development of a man of his time in the context of the culture and society from which he emerged and the individuals and places that shaped him. Marsh writes as an outsider, as the first of Bonhoeffer's major scholarly biographers who had not known the subject, and from outside Germany. He concentrates on the man and his personality, his inner life rather than his theology, though of course tracing the development of his theological writings in the context of his life.

A major focus of the book, explored with greater clarity than has been possible before, is Bonhoeffer's close and complex friendship with Eberhard Bethge, perhaps the most important relationship of his life other than with his family. In this and many other respects, Marsh does indeed add something to Bonhoeffer scholarship, and does so in a way that makes him accessible to those who might not want to engage with the intricacies of his theology or engage in guesswork about what he might have written had he lived longer. For explorations of Bonhoeffer's theology or indeed his ethics one will have to go elsewhere, but Marsh does offer a substantial and engaging model for the close relationship between theology and biography. He does not answer the question why Bonhoeffer continues to be such an attractive subject nor does he trace the history of the reception of this short life. Again this has been done elsewhere, for example in Stephen Haynes' *The Bonhoeffer Phenomenon*. But he does introduce his readers in a cunning and engaging way with the places associated with Bonhoeffer, the Berlin of the first half of the twentieth century, the expatriate communities of pre-war London and Barcelona, North

American theological scholarship in New York, a world away from the Bonhoeffer's alma maters of Tübingen and Berlin, as well as closer to home the illegal seminary of Finkenwalde that shaped *Life Together*.

Thus I would commend this book, possibly to be read before tackling Bethge and Schlingensiepen, or as a welcome complement to their work.

Natalie Watson, Peterborough

Christian Faith and Social Justice: Five Views

Vic McCracken
Bloomsbury, 2014, pp. 224, pbk, £17.99

Why is there such a divergence of views and approaches among Christians about the meaning of social justice, and what demands it places on Christians? This book provides a valuable approach to answering this, and the model could helpfully be used for other subjects. It starts out by narrating three situations for which Christians offer very different responses: the arrest of a gay couple in their home in Texas; the death of a 32-year-old lupus sufferer in Tennessee denied medical treatment because she was not insured; the expulsion from school of three Muslim girls in France for refusing to remove their *hijabs*. These instances are explored in the introductory chapter, in order to introduce the particular shape of the book.

That shape will be familiar to a North American audience, but less so to a British one. After the introduction, five authors each presents and defends a particular position on Christianity and social justice, with the other four each presenting a critique. This means that in reading the book not only do you gain insight into each of the five positions, but further insight into how the other authors contend with one another's ideas. The result is a rich series of challenges and arguments. While respondents frequently begin with the contention that the two positions are not as far apart as the author of the presenting essay seems to believe, they then go on to deal with the real differences. This method provides helpful methodological material for students of ethics trying to argue for or against a particular approach.

The editor and five authors are all North or Latin American, teaching in US universities or seminaries, with one exception who teaches in the UK. The five approaches they take are libertarianism,

Crucible January 2015

political liberalism, liberation theology, feminism and virtue ethics.

While I warmly commend the book, and it is engaging to read, I have three general comments about the book. First, there are some obvious gaps in this list of approaches, such as natural law and divine command. The editor tries to justify the gaps, but I think they are too wide. Second, at times I was unsure to what extent the essays or responses were engaging with the Christian dimension of the position presented. One of the authors in fact observes, 'Most if not all of the perspectives in this volume are products of unbelieving minds that had a "Christian hangover".' Third, the volume lacks a concluding essay by the author. His introduction is very helpful and clear. The book would benefit from a conclusion considering what has been learned through the shape and process it uses. That said, this is a stimulating volume that will be of particular value to students of Christian ethics and anyone trying to understand why Christians disagree on so many issues of social justice.

Martin Seeley, Westcott House, Cambridge

An Idol Unmasked: A Faith Perspective on Money

Peter Selby
Darton, Longman & Todd, 2014, pp.140, pbk, £10.99.

Peter Selby writes well. You can hear him speaking: articulate, intelligent, grammatical and passionate. Only twice did I have to re-read a sentence, when the main verb had strayed too far towards the end. This book is also well edited. These things need to be said, as they cannot be taken for granted nowadays. Reading *An Idol Unmasked* is a pleasurable experience.

Selby's earlier book, *Grace and Mortgage* (1997), is credited with having predicted the financial crisis of 2008. He warned then of the increasing and unsustainable levels of debt. Here he turns his attention to money itself, arguing that it has become an idol, a powerful influence on society and on individual lives. He warns that the virtually unregulated power of banks to lend far more than they hold on deposit, and the way in which money can be moved round the world instantly, have effectively turned money itself from being a tool to being the master to which even governments submit. He calls for a merciful economy, where people and their needs take central place, and in which careful planning and regulation depose Mammon in favour of mercy.

This is thoughtful polemic of high quality. Selby fires many arrows, most hitting legitimate targets. The growth of the lottery culture, and the particular vulnerability of the poor to the temptation of gambling, are good targets well struck. So too, to a large extent, are the capitulation of western governments to the power of money, and the failure to regulate the markets. The power of money to reproduce itself, the drive for quick high returns, the obscene levels of reward for those who gamble with other people's money, and the ever-widening gap between rich and poor, are analysed and targeted with precision.

Much of this has been said by others in recent years, but Selby makes interesting and fairly persuasive use of the Old Testament understanding of idols. Christians and secularists will benefit from thinking this through.

Some of Selby's targets are questionable, and his exegesis of four of Jesus' money parables is highly dubious. The suggestion that an emphasis on the numerical aspect of church growth is akin to subservience to Mammon is unwarranted. The call for a citizen's income for all, replacing welfare benefits, and paid for by much higher taxation, has never rung true as a way of encouraging societal stability. The removal of most sticks and the introduction of more carrots is also naively idealistic: telling me how much I enjoy television programmes, but with no threat of penalty, would not persuade me to pay a licence fee to watch game shows, soaps, singing and dancing competitions, or the promotion of celebrity.

And the tide is turning. West Germany's willingness to take a serious financial hit to allow reunification with East Germany, a general realization that unregulated markets cannot continue, and the Governor of the Bank of England's important speech at the June 2014 Inclusive Capitalism conference, all of which Selby mentions, actually demonstrate that the situation is not out of control in the way he claims. So does the Archbishop of Canterbury's invitation to be part of the October 2014 IMF/World Bank panel on Ethics and Finance.

This is an important and powerful book, but it must be read critically.

Donald Allister, Bishop of Peterborough

Crucible January 2015

Taking Stock of Bonhoeffer: Studies in Biblical Interpretation and Ethics

Stephen Plant
Ashgate, 2014, pp. 184, pbk, £19.99

Dietrich Bonhoeffer is one of the most important and most widely read theologians of the twentieth century, not only in his native Germany but also in the English-speaking world. He died at the relatively young age of 39 at the hands of the Nazis a month before the end of the Second World War, and the first translations of his work started appearing in the early 1950s. Bonhoeffer is read by many as a popular and accessible theologian, or should I say that what is read of his work are accessible texts such as *Life Together*, *Letters and Papers from Prison* and *The Cost of Discipleship*?, but has also attracted, and continues to attract, the attention of scholars worldwide.

Stephen Plant's collection of his own studies of Bonhoeffer's theology and ethics over a number of years belongs in the latter category. He offers close readings of a wide range of Bonhoeffer's texts, puts Bonhoeffer in dialogue with such conversation partners as the Methodist A. S. Peake, on reading Scripture, and the Roman Catholic ethicist and theologian William Cavanaugh on the sacrament of ethical reality. Yet, he also notices a certain reticence among British theologians to engage with Bonhoeffer, which is refreshing, given some of the uncritical readings of the writings of a man who is like any other of his own time and place: 'Bonhoeffer is a significant theologian whose life and thought belong to a rapidly receding past and his voice does not carry easily into contemporary theological conversation. The purpose of what follows is to enable a conversation between the living and the dead.' (p. 101)

So, is there anything new to say about Bonhoeffer, among the doyens of Christian ethics in the twentieth and twenty-first century? Or, is Bonhoeffer still any use, as he himself asked in set of short essays entitled 'After Ten Years' in 1943? In this book, Plant, one of very few English Bonhoeffer scholars for many years, maps his own engagement with Bonhoeffer and a wide range of aspects of his work, from his involvement in the German military counter intelligence, his encounters with members of other world faiths and other Christian churches to his engagement with the German philosopher Martin Heidegger, a supporter of the Nazi party. He completes the book with a short but masterly essay on 'Reading Bonhoeffer in Britain', which explores the aforementioned reticence among English, though not among Scottish, theologians, to engage with someone who was essentially trained as a systematic theologian in the best German tradition. He maps different phases of engagement and silence. Bonhoeffer was after all an Anglophile, lived and worked in London for a time and visited a number of centres of Anglican religious life in preparation not only for the community he later founded in Finkenwalde, the basis of *Life Together*, but also of a planned visit to an ashram in India, which never took place.

Plant emphasizes that Bonhoeffer advocates a worldly not secular theology which is yet deeply rooted in the Church and 'thus capable of integrating life in academy, church and world' (p. 161). Such a theology, Plant argues, and one is inclined to agree with him, could not only be attractive to English readers, but is also 'desperately needed', even in a context which in so many ways is very different from that in which Bonhoeffer lived, wrote and died. Thus Plant's book is an important contribution to the study of Bonhoeffer's work as we approach the seventieth anniversary of his death, and might also contribute to the development of a theology that reengages critically with the systematic tradition from which Bonhoeffer emerged.

Natalie Watson, Peterborough

The Deconstructed Church: Understanding Emerging Christianity

Gerardo Marti and Gladys Ganiel
Oxford University Press, 2014, pp. 268, hbk, £22.99

Ganiel and Marti have performed an important service to the wider Christian community by providing this first full length survey and analysis of the Emerging Church movement, although even calling it that suggests a coherence and level of organization that will not be uncovered by the evidence. Although many may have heard of Peter Rollins and Ikon, and the writings of Rob Bell and Brian McLaren, genuine encounter will probably not go much further than that. For those of us ensconced (trapped?) within the confines of institutional Christianity and struggling to translate this commitment into social and political activism, it is both heartening and challenging to hear the accounts of a new generation of Christians who have created different forms of church and social engagement, albeit with some clear links to the tradition in some cases.

As sociologists of religion, Ganiel and Marti have earthed their research in direct contact with the groups involved, and that is a real strength of the book. At the same time they have balanced this with an attempt to produce a theoretical framework in order to interpret and present their central argument, using particularly the work of Ulrich Beck in his book *A God of One's Own* (Polity Press, 2010) and his approach to the subject of individualization in contemporary culture. Their argument is that the evidence suggests that what is happening in these various groups will be sustained over time and is a serious and enduring way of exercising the Christian faith, rather than a fad or passing fashion. Although many appear to be seeking refuge from aspects of traditional church life, especially its more evangelical components, this is more than a protest movement and has a life and integrity of its own. Although also it seems to appeal mostly to a younger, white, middle class constituency who might find such a way of being church more challenging once family commitments impinge, they believe that it does attract a wider range of people. So what are the characteristics of Emerging Church?

Chapter 1 provides some snapshots, such as pub churches (pp. 11–14); emerging Christian conferences (pp. 14–17); online networks (pp. 17–18) and neo-monasticism (pp. 19–21) and then presents the historical context for this.

Chapter 2 takes us directly into some of the examples of what the authors call pluralist congregations, and we get a feel for their normal activities. Who are the people attending though? Their response: '.... very few people in emerging congregations come from atheistic or agnostic backgrounds. Instead, emerging congregations are a haven for the "dechurched" those who had a religious upbringing but had grown disillusioned with conventional religious institutions' (p. 40). What are the attractions of this alternative? Apparently greater freedom of belief and practice, 'belief held lightly', as Katharine Moody describes it (p. 43); an acceptance of difference which they describe, using Beck, as 'religious cosmopolitanism' (p. 44); a non-judgementalism and general level of informality and flexibility. Despite the emphasis upon the individual discovering and working out 'their own salvation', belonging to a community or congregation is still a vital component of the process, along with a willingness to become involved in local areas through direct social action. As the authors note, this does not meet with unconditional approval as some find the lack of boundaries and low levels of traditional organization too much of a challenge (pp. 51–4).

Chapter 3 examines the idea of a Christian identity and the real difficulties that individuals have faced in splitting from their former churches and redefining themselves. The argument is that this is not simply a striving for an 'authentic self', but an enactment of a 'legitimized religious self' (p. 77). Emerging Christians are attempting to renegotiate the rules of the broader system of Christianity and, in the process are actively negotiating their own religious selves. This would seem to rely on what could be seen as a postmodern understanding of what it is to be, or become human, which challenges the notion of a core, unchanging self.

Chapter 4 is equally fascinating and focusses on the role of conversation and narrative within the groups. Here the authors draw again upon the theories of Beck and Giddens and their notion of reflexivity (p. 81), although one needs to note that along with Scott Lash, they have between them rather different understandings of the concept, and that some of us have a rather less optimistic view and believe there are limits to reflexivity (see *Christianity and the New Social Order: Manifesto for a Fairer Future*, Atherton, Baker and Reader, eds, SPCK, 2011, Chapter 1 by Reader looking at Habermas's use of reflexivity). I note also that other interpreters quoted such as Packard and Sanders refer to the changes as 'lines of flight' quoting Deleuze and Guattari in the context of how emerging Christians try to free themselves from the suffocating effects of late modern corporatization in churches (p. 82). I suppose of as much interest of the groups themselves are the contemporary sociological and philosophical sources that many of us now employ in our interpretations of what is developing. I would have used Bruno Latour in this context and his idea of keeping the references circulating rather than trying to impose or establish a definitive religious truth, as well as the relational Christian realism some of us are working on as another way of contextualizing and making sense of emerging church. Packard and Sanders talk about the messiness of what is happening, whereas some of us use instead the discourse of blurred encounters or entangled fidelities (p. 108), but it seems as though we share a general understanding nevertheless.

Chapter 5 looks at the deconstruction of congregational practices and reactions against the megachurches in the US mainline denominational practices elsewhere. It is clear that many familiar elements of worship are maintained though, prayer, singing, reference to scripture and teaching (p. 111). Communitarian preaching is a really interesting and important development where those gathered are participants rather than passive consumers or members of an audience (p. 114). Peter Rollins works on a rather different approach as a 'provocateur', and Katharine Moody again has done some interesting and creative work on this (p. 116). Another aspect of organization which differs from most institutional Christianity is a 'flat leadership structure', decentralized, egalitarian, spontaneous and relational (p. 119). There is of course another side to this in that removing the persona of the priest as the focus of activity may just create a vacuum into which step the more charismatic figures of leaders such as Rollins and Bell, but there is an awareness of this, and attempts to counteract what often becomes an inevitable development over time. I wonder the extent to which the flat hierarchies require the flat ontology which relational Christian realism see as essential?

Chapter 6 follows the movements into direct action, into the work of the neo-monastic communities and 'temporary autonomous zones' (pp. 153–6), and looks at how adherents try to put their faith into practice. The final chapter returns more systematically to the tasks of interpretation and builds upon the concepts of 'collective institutional entrepreneurship' (p. 163); 'religious individualization' (p. 164), and faces the criticism that the movement is actually colluding with the forces of capitalism that it claims to eschew. Others who feature in the analysis are Heelas and Woodhead and their theory of the turn to the subjective from the earlier Kendal project, Castells' writings on the network society, as well as Bauman, Beck, Giddens and Lynch (p. 180). They acknowledge that the use of the term deconstruction which philosophically is identified with Derrida is here being employed more sociologically and describes a process in which emerging Christians are redefining their relationships with existing structures in order to develop a different religious orientation (p. 193). An appendix goes into more detail of the research methodology, which is a helpful addition.

I commend this book as both an important resource for understanding emerging church, but also as a source of interpretative tools with which to engage these exciting and challenging developments. As with the movement itself, of great interest is what now follows, both in terms of practical activity and theoretical analysis.

John Reader, Ironstone Benefice and William Temple Foundation

Anglican Social Theology: Renewing the Vision Today

Edited by Malcolm Brown with Jonathan Chaplin, John Hughes, Anna Rowlands and Alan Suggate, Foreword by The Archbishop of Canterbury,
Church House Publishing, 2014, pp. 226, £19.99

Crucible January 2015

There are many good reasons for publishing a book like this just now. Post-Crash, in the aftermath of the enthusiasm for the Big (or was it Good?) Society, watching the cracks appear ever more discernibly in the Welfare state, the questions multiply: where are we, the church, in all this? Who are 'we'? Does that 'who' have any coherent identity? What can we offer?

There have been some important attempts to set down some possible answers to these questions recently. Of course, they are not all Anglican. (The Anglicanism with which we're dealing in this book is that of the Church of England. This is explicable: it is a church with a history of social theology and it is the local church for most of the contributors. It suffices to say, this book doesn't pretend to speak for everyone everywhere.) Benedict XVI's important encyclicals on love, human development and civil economy are good examples of lively contributions to the debate. Rowan Williams – whom most of the contributors treat in various illuminating ways   is an influential figure. Pope Francis and the current Archbishop of Canterbury have made more recent practical and charismatic contributions. Recent Anglican academic theology – much of it politically, socially and culturally attentive – is also building up an increasingly large library that needs to be made more 'available' to practitioners. But of course the majority of Anglicans contributions come from laity and clergy doing – quietly or loudly – what Anglicans do in their own jobs, as volunteers and as local communities. It just so happens that this is so much more visible in the current climate.

Anglican Social Theology is a taking stock. It takes the form of a colloquium. Three Anglicans from different traditions set our their stalls and Malcolm Brown, Director of Mission and Public Affairs for the Archbishop's Council, sets the scene and then offers some concluding reflections. Anna Rowlands (a Roman Catholic) contributes as an interested observer of the Anglican tradition.

This is not a reader in Anglican social theology nor does it offer fulsome descriptions of the history of Anglican social theology. There is some more extended attention paid to some figures (William Temple,

Rowan Williams) and descriptions of more recent theologies but you won't find lengthy descriptions of Charles Gore, the Christendom movement or F. D. Maurice here. The closest we get to that is Alan Suggate's extended treatment of Temple and Anna Rowlands' fascinating comparison of 1937's *The Churches Survey Their Task* and 1931's *Quadragesimo anno*.

Instead, this is a polite conversation but not one without conviction. This is a great strength of the book. Conviction is not something that the various branches of Anglicanism – at home and abroad – tend to lack (thank goodness) but we're not very good at listening. This book suggests that the contributors have respectfully paid some focussed attention to one another.

As the conversation shows, Anglican social theology is not an uncontested phenomenon. The irenic tone here hides some of the more vexed disagreements evident more widely between social theologies today. For example, there is a keen dispute at the moment over the relative benefits of the discourse of the common good. Is common good language important because it reveals a shared belief that there may be such a thing as a common good, however elusive, in our age of managerialism and utilitarianism – when politics is a technique for balancing irreconcilable and competing goods and schooling is seen as just a means of producing financially viable citizens? Or, does the common good project hide bids for cultural hegemony by powerful actors at the expense of healthy pluralism?

There are also quite stark differences over what we see to be the purpose of government and state structures. Are state structures tragically necessary in a fallen world to balance power and to restrain violence by using coercion? Or, is human association a pre-lapsarian good, in which even the modern state can dimly participate as it seeks to guarantee the flourishing of civil society? Is government a mechanism for managing the co-existence of rival claims and goods or dare we hope that such goods in creation might be reconciled as the world is being redeemed? Should the Church cede matters of government and social ordering to the proper secular agencies, or should the church abandon the state to its fallenness, or is the Church there to remind the state that it is accountable to something beyond? The contested interpretation of Augustine of Hippo looms large over the conversation. These questions are all being debated and intimately impinge on how the Church of England acts at every level.

Listening to the conversation in the book, tidy compartmentalisations are troubled. Alan Suggate's appraisal of the Temple tradition reminds us that Temple, unlike Reinhold Niebuhr with whom he is often associated, was an ecclesiastical thinker animated by a rich sacramental theology. He had an ecumenical interest in adapting Catholic Social Teaching to an Anglican matrix. He was not just interested in the Church's relationship to the state or the formation of individual Christian citizens but had an abiding desire to see the flourishing of intermediate institutions in civil society too.

Whilst Jonathan Chaplin admits that evangelicalism has been better at social action than social theology, he reminds us that there are a number of heavy-weight evangelical theologians who would resource this tradition as it seeks to articulate the theology that stands behind its activism. He points to the importance of scriptural *narrative* (often less evident in other traditions) and how the work of interpretation is something that we can do together. He also notes the ecumenical possibilities of evangelicalism, which could lead to the exporting of our best work to other traditions (and vice versa).

Anna Rowlands helps us to see what is distinctively Anglican by comparing its social theologies to Catholic Social Teaching. She notes that by comparison to Roman Catholic thought Anglicanism has often over-theologised the state and the nation. She also picks up the lack of attention paid to important female voices and the loss of the laity in the rather clericalist bias of the 'Church speaks to the nation' model. Her discussion of the church's relationship to the state is particularly helpful. From her particular vantage point in the 'colloquium' she is able (and dares) to offer a constructive social theology that is insightful and reveals that it is not a lonely enterprise; we are amongst friends.

As we listen to John Hughes' account of the recent renewal of Anglican social theology after Temple we hear that – contrary to popular opinion – it is not just about having a second bite at the Neo-Orthodox cherry. John Hughes was killed in a road accident just before the publication of the book, and it was a personal tragedy for his very many friends (who span the theological traditions) but also for the Church of England. We see in this essay a fragment of his wider project to renew an 'integral Christian humanism'. It would be fitting if one aspect of his legacy would be the putting to bed of the idea that ecclesial theologians of the post-Temple tradition (e.g., John Milbank, the radically orthodox, Stanley Hauerwas) are simply world-denying, revelatory positivists who are sectarian and tribalist, refusing to engage with other disciplines and communities. For this reason, Hughes' project bears discussing at greater length.

Crucible January 2015

Hughes' essay shows why it is dishonest to characterize this tradition in this way. He argues that for this post-Temple tradition human association is theologically primary. It is in *community* that peace, which is the gift of the risen Jesus, is known.

For all the laudable gains of liberalism it tends to operate at the level of the individual or the state. It is concerned less with the spheres of actual human living – those intermediate institutions and associations where life is lived. (Compare Ofsted's rather formal and universal list of British Values – rule of law, freedom of speech, individual liberty – to what British people actually get up for in the morning.) Once you make *association* theologically primary then you are likely to pay attention – joyfully and critically – to lived humanity in all its glory and gory detail.

Whilst radical orthodoxy is often taken to task for its critique of the 'secular', what it has in its sights – as John shows – is its supposed neutrality. Secularisms have their own (often concealed and unacknowledged) social ontologies. They may be better or worse but they are never neutral. Which is to say, secular experts of whatever kind have their own axes to grind, as do theologians. The post-Temple tradition is deeply concerned with the secular, if we mean by that the time that we call the everyday. It is the way we inhabit that time, our lived practices, that make it what it is. In secular time, we find churches establishing foodbanks, promoting credit unions, brokering relationships with the public and private sectors, working with children's centres, celebrating festivals, worshipping, supporting the living wage, forming Christian disciples, advising on governmental policy and seeking to civilize the economy. One of the often ignored triumphs of this renewal of social theology is the potential it evinces for a theology of the laity. The Christian practice of the people of God – individually, locally and corporately – has beneficial effects in a pluralistic environment.

Hughes' integral Christian humanism believes that in a created world, there is nothing human to which we should not pay attention. It argues that grace is not seen apart from nature. Neither is it something that arrives from without after the fact. Grace works from within perfecting and transforming. It attests to a creation that is already a grace and which is ordered to glory. As such, the theological is not an add on but integral to the world. So Hughes argues that church reports with a theological coda to a sociological analysis don't hit the mark. Hughes praises Benedict XVI for speaking about 'development' in a theological idiom using the language of love and also speaking of the economy in terms of gift. We can even use language that doesn't sound theological and still be theological through and through. Hughes praises the work of political phenomena like Blue Labour and ResPublica, both supported by theologians and ecclesiasts, who are offering visions of civil economy, personal virtue and public honour in terms, whilst not explicitly theological, chime with a theological vision and Christian practices.

Integral Christian humanism does not see the church in the world as a bastion of purity. It is where sin is made visible because it is confessed and we can actually *see* redemption at work. In a fallen world, the work of grace must first of all look like redemption before it looks like further glorification. This means that this renewal of social theology is finally more hopeful than it is critical. It articulates a fully theological vision that is at home in a fallen but potentially glorious world.

Malcolm Brown helpfully sets the context of current Anglican social theology in his introduction, explores its contemporary importance, and brokers the conversation that follows. In his conclusion he is more strategic, as one would hope, and asks whether there is such a thing as Anglican social theology and what it looks like. Unsurprisingly, the answer is rather, well, Anglican. Ours is a rich, capacious tradition. It is in itself a conversation but, more than that, it is a set of practices that are ceaselessly important. This book is just the beginning of longer, more detailed conversations. It points to the need for attention to the history of our social theology, more ecumenical, ethnographic and interdisciplinary work, and – very much so – the need to listen to one another. It is a profound regret that we cannot listen to John Hughes in personal encounter but his legacy, as one who loved theology and social life, is a grace that we can cherish and an inspiration to continue the work of Anglican social theology.

Matthew Bullimore, Vicar of Royston and Priest
in Charge of Felkirk in the Diocese of Leeds

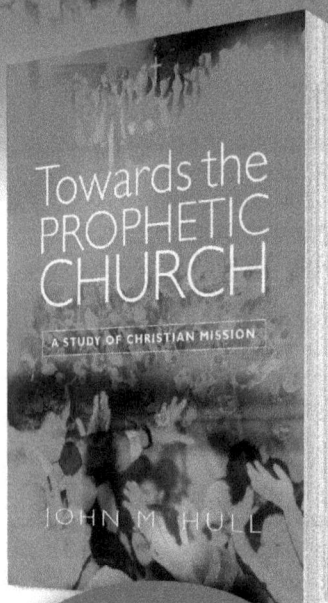

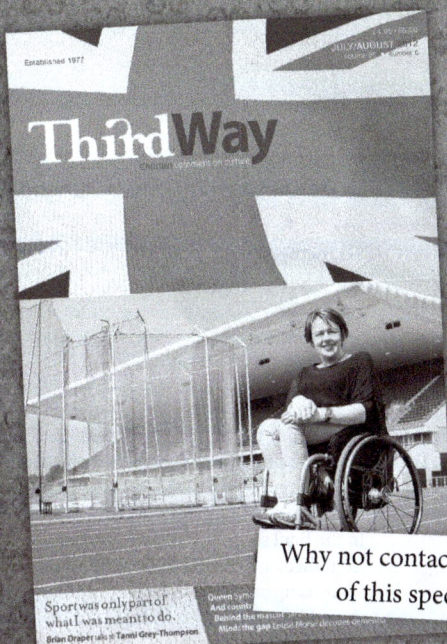